# ALL'S WELL THAT ENDS WELL
# & THE MERRY WIVES OF WINDSOR

## NOTES

including
- *Life of Shakespeare*
- *Introductions*
- *Brief Plot Summaries*
- *Lists of Characters*
- *Summaries and Commentaries*
- *Questions for Review*
- *Selected Bibliographies*

*by*
*Denis Calandra, Ph.D.*
*Department of Theater*
*University of South Florida*

**Cliffs Notes**
**INCORPORATED**

LINCOLN. NEBRASKA   68501

**Editor**

Gary Carey, M.A.
University of Colorado

**Consulting Editor**

*James L. Roberts, Ph.D.*
*Department of English*
*University of Nebraska*

Cliffs Notes, Inc.          Lincoln, Nebraska

# CONTENTS

# THE MERRY WIVES OF WINDSOR

# ALL'S WELL THAT ENDS WELL & MERRY WIVES OF WINDSOR Notes

## LIFE OF SHAKESPEARE

Many books have assembled facts, reasonable suppositions, traditions, and speculations concerning the life and career of William Shakespeare. Taken as a whole, these materials give a rather comprehensive picture of England's foremost dramatic poet. Tradition and sober supposition are not necessarily false because they lack proved bases for their existence. It is important, however, that persons interested in Shakespeare should distinguish between *facts* and *beliefs* about his life.

From one point of view, modern scholars are fortunate to know as much as they do about a man of middle-class origin who left a small country town and embarked on a professional career in sixteenth-century London. From another point of view, they know surprisingly little about the writer who has continued to influence the English language and its drama and poetry for more than three hundred years. Sparse and scattered as these facts of his life are, they are sufficient to prove that a man from Stratford by the name of William Shakespeare wrote the major portion of the thirty-seven plays which scholars ascribe to him. The concise review which follows will concern itself with some of these records.

No one knows the exact date of William Shakespeare's birth. His baptism occurred on Wednesday, April 26, 1564. His father was John Shakespeare, tanner, glover, dealer in grain, and town official of Stratford; his mother, Mary, was the daughter of Robert Arden, a prosperous gentleman-farmer. The Shakespeares lived on Henley Street.

Under a bond dated November 28, 1582, William Shakespeare and Anne Hathaway entered into a marriage contract. The baptism of their eldest child, Susanna, took place in Stratford in May, 1583. One year and nine months later their twins, Hamnet and Judith, were christened in the same church. The parents named them for the poet's friends, Hamnet and Judith Sadler.

Early in 1596, William Shakespeare, in his father's name, applied to the College of Heralds for a coat of arms. Although positive proof is lacking, there is reason to believe that the Heralds granted this request, for in 1599 Shakespeare again made application for the right to quarter his coat of arms with that of his mother. Entitled to her father's coat of arms, Mary had lost this privilege when she married John Shakespeare before he held the official status of gentleman.

In May of 1597, Shakespeare purchased New Place, the outstanding residential property in Stratford at that time. Since John Shakespeare had suffered financial reverses prior to this date, William must have achieved success for himself.

Court records show that in 1601-02, William Shakespeare began rooming in the household of Christopher Mountjoy in London. Subsequent disputes over the wedding settlement and agreement between Mountjoy and his son-in-law, Stephen Belott, led to a series of legal actions, and in 1612 the court scribe recorded Shakespeare's deposition of testimony relating to the case.

In July, 1605, William Shakespeare paid four hundred and forty pounds for the lease of a large portion of the tithes on certain real estate in and near Stratford. This was an arrangement whereby Shakespeare purchased half the annual tithes, or taxes, on certain agricultural products from parcels of land in and near Stratford. In addition to receiving approximately ten per cent income on his investment, he almost doubled his capital. This was possibly the most important and successful investment of his lifetime, and it paid a steady income for many years.

Shakespeare is next mentioned when John Combe, a resident of Stratford, died on July 12, 1614. To his friend, Combe bequeathed the sum of five pounds. These records and similar ones are important, not because of their economic significance but because they prove the existence of William Shakespeare in Stratford and in London during this period.

On March 25, 1616, William Shakespeare revised his last will and testament. He died on April 23 of the same year. His body lies within the chancel and before the altar of the Stratford church. A rather wry inscription is carved upon his tombstone:

> Good Friend, for Jesus' sake, forbear
> To dig the dust enclosed here;
> Blest be the man that spares these stones
> And curst be he who moves my bones.

The last direct descendant of William Shakespeare was his grand-daughter, Elizabeth Hall, who died childless in 1670.

These are the most outstanding facts about Shakespeare the man, as apart from those about the dramatist and poet. Such pieces of information, scattered from 1564 through 1616, declare the existence of such a person, not as a writer or actor, but as a private citizen. It is illogical to think that anyone would or could have fabricated these details for the purpose of deceiving later generations.

In similar fashion, the evidence establishing William Shakespeare as the foremost playwright of his day is positive and persuasive. Robert Greene's *Groatsworth of Wit,* in which he attacked Shakespeare, a mere actor, for presuming to write plays in competition with Greene and his fellow playwrights, was entered in the *Stationers' Register* on September 20, 1592. In 1594 Shakespeare acted before Queen Elizabeth, and in 1594-95 his name appeared as one of the shareholders of the Lord Chamberlain's Company. Francis Meres in his *Palladis Tamia* (1598) called Shakespeare "mellifluous and hony-tongued" and compared his comedies and tragedies with those of Plautus and Seneca in excellence.

Shakespeare's continued association with Burbage's company is equally definite. His name appears as one of the owners of the Globe in 1599. On May 19, 1603, he and his fellow actors received a patent from James I designating them as the King's Men and making them Grooms of the Chamber. Late in 1608 or early in 1609, Shakespeare and his colleagues purchased the Blackfriars Theatre and began using it as their winter location when weather made production at the Globe inconvenient.

Other specific allusions to Shakespeare, to his acting and his writing, occur in numerous places. Put together, they form irrefutable testimony that William Shakespeare of Stratford and London was the leader among Elizabethan playwrights.

One of the most impressive of all proofs of Shakespeare's author-ship of his plays is the First Folio of 1623, with the dedicatory verse which appeared in it. John Heminge and Henry Condell, members of Shakespeare's own company, stated that they collected and issued the plays as a memorial to their fellow actor. Many contemporary poets contributed eulogies to Shakespeare; one of the best-known of these poems is by Ben Jonson, a fellow actor and, later, a friendly rival. Jonson also criticized Shakespeare's dramatic work in *Timber: or, Discoveries* (1641).

Certainly there are many things about Shakespeare's genius and career which the most diligent scholars do not know and cannot explain, but the facts which do exist are sufficient to establish Shakespeare's identity as a man and his authorship of the thirty-seven plays which reputable critics acknowledge to be his.

# ALL'S WELL THAT ENDS WELL

## INTRODUCTION

It is difficult to assign a date to the composition of *All's Well*. There are no definite allusions or associations with contemporary slang or happenings. There are a good number of rimed couplets, suggesting that this play might be an early work of Shakespeare's. But because these couplets are such fine examples, they suggest a mastery of the couplet tradition instead of immaturity. Most scholars who note errors in characterization, as well as entrance and exit notations, seem to think that this First Folio edition is probably a recast, rewritten version of the play, lacking Shakespeare's final editing. And because of one of its key lines, they think that it may be a "lost play" of Shakespeare's – *Love's Labour's Won*.

Shakespeare's plot of a beautiful woman who is turned down by the man whom she loves – after she has cured a king of a critical illness – is clearly taken from William Painter's *Palace of Pleasure* (1566), a situation that had already been explored by Boccaccio in his *Decameron;* both stories also contain the ingenious "bed trick." At that time, Helena's cleverness in getting a child from Bertram would have been applauded. The baby would have been proof of her deep love and courage. It was sterling – if ironic – proof of her vow of fidelity. Then, as well as today, Bertram would have had few redeeming qualities. He lacks all sense of honor; he is a cad. Thus, the comedy is ultimately flawed. We cannot totally rejoice at Helena's "success" in regaining her husband. The play simply has a rapid "happy ending," which was required. Ultimately, we feel that Helena is such a remarkable woman that her absolute infatuation with a fraud makes her character suspect. The meaning of *All's Well* is, therefore, ambiguous and seemingly ironic.

## BRIEF PLOT SUMMARY

The central action of *All's Well That Ends Well* concerns Helena, a beautiful woman, and her pursuit of a man of higher social position than herself in the French court of Rousillon. Helena is the daughter of a recently deceased court physician; the man whom she pursues is Bertram, a young man of the nobility, who is in mourning for his late father, the Count.

Helena follows Bertram to Paris where, as a reward for "miraculously" curing the king of an apparently terminal illness, she is granted the husband of her choice. She chooses Bertram. Bertram at first refuses to have her, but then he submits to the angry king's command – but only outwardly. Together with his dubious "follower" Parolles, Bertram flees France to fight in the Italian wars, where he plans to achieve the necessary "honor" suitable to his rank. Furthermore, he vows never to consummate his marriage with Helena unless she can perform two "impossible" tasks: (1) "get the ring upon [which is on] my finger," and (2) "show me a child begotten of thy body that I am father to." Helena does just that, with the help of a widow (whom she pays handsomely) and the widow's virgin daughter, Diana. During the well-known "bed trick," Bertram is fooled into believing that he has made love to Diana, whereas, in reality, Helena has smuggled herself into the bed. An exchange of rings also takes place. Diana and Helena continue the ruse until the last minutes of the play, when they surprise the entire Parisian court (who think that Helena is dead), and they then embarrass Bertram deeply when they reveal what has transpired. But Helena finally has her man, and "all" has apparently ended "well."

In a comical subplot, another "trick" is used, this time to reveal Parolles' dishonesty in the presence of Bertram; Parolles is taken captive, blindfolded, and outrageous denunciations are extracted from him about Bertram and others. But even Parolles is grudgingly accepted back into the company at the end of the play. Again, "all's well that ends well" – apparently.

# LIST OF CHARACTERS

## Helena

The daughter of a very famous, recently deceased court physician, Helena has the physical and mental attributes which could command the attention of virtually any eligible bachelor, but unfortunately, she does not have the correct social pedigree to entice the man whom she loves, Bertram, a Count's son. Through the use of her native wit and the body of knowledge which she inherits from her father, as well as because of her sheer strength of will, she overcomes all obstacles and wins Bertram. To some commentators on this play, Helena's tactics seem questionable, although no one underestimates her strength of character.

## Bertram

For several reasons, Bertram seems significantly inferior to Helena. He is under the influence of the patently superficial Parolles, and he lies outright on more than one occasion. Furthermore, he blatantly disregards the king's wishes. To a twentieth-century audience, he might seem to have every right to refuse a forced marriage, but to the world which the play inhabits, that is not the case. Besides, Helena is clearly (in everyone else's opinion) a splendid person. The play ends, however, in such an abrupt manner that Shakespeare leaves us wondering just how "well" all has "ended" for Bertram and his "rightful" bride.

## King of France

In his prime, the king was a valiant warrior and a staunch friend of Bertram's father. He is utterly charmed by Helena, and he is grateful for the cure which she administers to him. All of this makes his outrage even greater when Bertram refuses to accept Helena as a bride. He exerts his royal authority to force the marriage, and in Shakespeare's scheme of things in the play, he seems to be right in doing so.

## Countess of Rousillon

Bertram's mother fully sympathizes with Helena in her state of lovelorn agony, and she goes so far as to say that she will disown her son as a result of his rejection of her adopted "daughter." She does what she can to make things "end well."

## Lafeu

Lafeu is an elderly friend of the Countess and her family. His role is that of adviser and mollifier. He is the first to see through Parolles' schemes, and it is his daughter whose planned marriage to Bertram (before Helena is "resurrected" at the end of the play) will signal a return to good order.

## Parolles

Lafeu sums up the character of Parolles when he says: "The soul of this man is his clothes." Parolles is the tempter of Bertram as a "prodigal son," and in the end, Parolles is seen as such and rejected.

## Clown (Lavache)

The Countess' servant offers comic reflections about several characters in the play, most pointedly about Parolles. His mouth is lewd, and his manner is absurd.

## A Widow of Florence

For a fee, the widow helps Helena arrange and execute the old "bed trick"; here, Bertram is trapped into sleeping with his own wife in the belief that she is another woman.

## Diana

Diana is the widow's daughter and Helena's ally in her pursuit of Bertram. She is the bait used to trap Bertram. Diana displays a good deal of wit and a composed bearing under the pressure of the courtly observers during the final "revelation scene."

## Mariana

A neighbor of the widow.

## Two French Lords, the Brothers Dumain

The two noblemen who mastermind the plot to expose Parolles. They are friends to Bertram.

# SUMMARIES AND COMMENTARIES

## ACT I – SCENE 1

### Summary

At the opening of this play, the main figures of the plot are weighed down with thoughts of two recent deaths. "Young Bertram," the Count of Rousillon (in France), has lost his father, as has Helena, the beautiful daughter of a famed physician, Gerard de Narbon, "whose skill was almost as great as his honesty." Bertram's mother is further distressed that she must say farewell to her son, now a ward of the ailing king of France. Opening the play, she exclaims: "In delivering my son from me [to the king's court], I bury a second husband." As an older lord and a close family friend, Lafeu assures the Countess that in the king she shall find someone as good as a second husband for herself and a second father for Bertram.

Once mother and son have said their goodbyes and he has departed, Helena delivers a soliloquy in which she reveals a double reason for her sadness. "I am undone; there is no living, none, if Bertram be away. . . ." A "follower" of Bertram, named Parolles, interrupts her and engages her in an extended dialogue on the subject of virginity. He pledges that he will "return a perfect courtier" from Paris, where he is about to go with Bertram. A second soliloquy, this time by Helena, reveals her to be resolute in her pledge to pursue her unlikely attempt at capturing Bertram's heart: ". . . my project may deceive me, but my intents are fixed, and will not leave me."

# Commentary

A gloomy mood at the opening of the play is often customary for a Shakespearean comedy. But amidst the general lamentation over departures and deaths, there is some emotional ambiguity which sets a tone for this "problem play," as *All's Well* has been called by some critics. Lafeu remarks on Helena's tears at the Countess' praise, whereupon the older woman kindly says that Helena must *not* cry lest people think that she is "affecting" or putting on her sad demeanor. Helena's answer – "I do affect a sorrow indeed, but I have it too" – seems puzzling, until we learn in her soliloquy that she is crying for the sake of her unacknowledged lover, and not (or not entirely) for her deceased father. Helena keeps to herself much of the time, partly because she may be embarrassed at the feelings she has for a person beyond her station, socially. In the first moments of the play, she is uneasy, aware that Bertram is "so far above me."

One wonders what Bertram's feelings in this first scene may be. Though some editors have disputed the placement of Lafeu's second line in the following exchange, it seems possible that the wise, older gentleman is reacting to Bertram's abruptness in cutting off his mother's speech.

> *Lafeu:* Moderate lamentation is the right of the
> dead,
> Excessive grief the enemy to the living.
> *Countess:* If the living be enemy to the grief,
> The excess makes it soon mortal.
> *Bertram:* Madam, I desire your holy wishes.
> *Lafeu:* How understand we that?
>
> (64–69)

There is something of a gentle handslap in the tone of Lafeu's last line. Bertram may be speaking rudely, overstepping the quite normal impatience of a young man about to leave home (and to leave off mourning) for a more adventuresome life in Paris. Consider for yourself if this line – "How understand we that?" – makes sense here, or if it might better fit in just before the words "moderate lamentation," where some editors place it.

There is an abrupt shift in tone at Parolles' entrance. Helena confides that he is a "notorious liar" whom she tolerates only because of his association with Bertram. The conversation between the two, saturated in polite obscenity, gives the audience a clear view of the play's heroine as someone who is not so romantic and frail that she cannot survive in the gritty world of court sexuality. Parolles argues conventionally that virginity is nonsensical since it goes against nature and since it condemns, as it were, its own mother, and furthermore, he says that it loses its value proportionately with age. Helena can bandy easily enough with this affected man of the world and can ask in her own private interest, "How might one do, sir, to lose it [one's virginity] to her own liking?" But her mind is fixed on Bertram, for he will soon appear at court in Paris. Notice the way that her lines are broken to indicate breathlessness and distraction as she imagines Bertram there amidst pretty mistresses:

> . . . with a world of pretty, fond, adoptious chris-
> tendoms [young women with adopted names] that
> blinking Cupid gossips [*i.e.*, that the god of love god-
> fathers]. Now shall he—I know not what he shall.
> God send him well! The court's a learning place, and
> he is one—
>
> (187–92)

Helena insults Parolles, calling him a coward and an overdressed fool, and he beats a hasty retreat. Her feistiness is evident.

Helena's second soliloquy differs from the first in its view of fate. Now the focus is on individual determination.

> Our remedies oft in ourselves do lie,
> Which we ascribe to heaven. The fated sky
>     [influence of the stars]
> Gives us free scope; only doth backward pull
> Our slow designs when we ourselves are dull.
>
> (231–34)

The exchange between Helena and Parolles seems to have had the effect of bolstering her courage.

# ACT I – SCENE 2

## Summary

Bertram presents himself at court in Paris just as the king is bidding his soldiers to fight in the Italian wars. The sight of Bertram, Lafeu, and Parolles spurs memories of former days:

> I would I had that corporal soundness now,
> As when thy father and myself in friendship
> First tried our soldiership!
>
> (24–26)

At the end of this short scene, the king asks how long it has been since the court physician at Rousillon died; if he were still alive – perhaps he could cure the king's illness.

## Commentary

Shakespeare broadly contrasts youth and age here, with Bertram greeting the feeble king while preparations are made for a war in which the young gentlemen of France can prove themselves. Note that the war is described as being more a training ground than anything else: ". . . freely have they leave/ To stand on either part" means they can fight for either Siena or Florence, as far as the king is concerned. In this play, "honor" has a number of different connotations, one of which is the prestige a young man like Bertram can achieve in battle.

One remark which the king makes in describing Bertram's father has a bearing on the previous scene. The king says:

> Who were below him he used as creatures of another
>     place,
> And bowed his eminent top to their low ranks,
> Making them proud of his humility,
> In their poor praise he humbled.
>
> (42–45)

The gist of the comment is that Bertram's father was *not* a social snob. Ironically, a motivating factor in Bertram's behavior toward Helena (whom we know to be sensitive to the issue) is just such snobbery.

# ACT I – SCENE 3

## Summary

The clown Lavache begs the Countess for permission to marry Isbel for the simple reason that he is "driven on by the flesh." The Countess listens to his facetious and cynical logic concerning marriage, and then playfully (though this will change), she remonstrates with him: "Wilt thou ever be a foul-mouthed and calumnious knave?"

In the second part of the scene, the Countess' steward informs her that he has overheard Helena, who thought she was alone, saying that "she loved your son." "Keep it to yourself," is the Countess' advice, adding, "Many likelihoods informed me of this before. . . ." Helena enters and when confronted with the fact – "You love my son" – she begs pardon. But, to her surprise, she receives Bertram's mother's blessing in her endeavor – "Thou shalt have my leave and love" – and so Helena makes plans to go to Paris with a remedy "to cure the desperate languishings whereof/ The King is rendered lost." Of course, her plan is also to pursue the man she loves.

## Commentary

In the encounter with the clown, the Countess engages in explicit sexual talk, just as Helena did with Parolles. Shakespeare's clowns, of course, had license to say things which smack of the other side of respectability, but these two scenes which depict refined women at ease with the language of obscene puns and innuendoes give a strong impression of the very real sexual matter at the heart of *All's Well That Ends Well*.

The steward's description of Helena, who expressed herself "in the most bitter touch of sorrow that e'er I heard virgin exclaim in," moves the Countess to reflect on her own past romantic involvements:

> Even so it was with me, when I was young;
> If ever we are nature's, these [pains] are ours; this
>     thorn
> Doth to our rose of youth rightly belong;
> Our blood [passion] to us, this to our blood is born.
>
> (134–37)

This observation, and the affection it implies for Helena, parallels the scene between Bertram and the King of France, where age views youth with compassion and understanding. Helena's tortured evasiveness (she doesn't want to be considered the Countess' daughter and therefore merely Bertram's "sister") is matched by her pluck. She describes herself as coming from "poor but honest" stock and will not "have him [Bertram] till I do deserve him," for—as yet—she hasn't singlemindedly made an effort to pursue him. However, the idea of going to Paris with a secret remedy of her father's to cure the king was surely prompted by her desire to follow Bertram. She impresses the Countess enormously by the end of the scene. Some critics have been less sympathetic to Helena, viewing her as merely a clever fortune-hunter who lays her plans in these early scenes. Is there any justification for that view?

## ACT II – SCENE 1

**Summary**

In Paris, the king wishes his young warriors well as they leave for the Italian wars: ". . . be you the sons/ Of worthy Frenchmen . . . see that you come/ Not to woo honor, but to wed it." He adds a sly note to "beware the Italian women!" Bertram, who is unhappy that he must linger behind—and be told that he is "too young" and that he must wait until "the next year"—succumbs to Parolles' and the other lords' urging to steal away on his own, for "there's honour in the theft."

Lafeu and the king now exchange formal greetings, and the Rousillon elder statesman politely urges the king to shake off despair:

> . . . O, will you eat no grapes, my royal fox?
> Yes, but you will my noble grapes . . . if my royal fox
> Could reach them. I have seen a medicine
> That's able to breathe life into a stone.
>
> (72–75)

Soon, Lafeu introduces Helena, "Doctor She," who explains her presence and describes her deceased father's special cure:

> And, hearing your high majesty is touched

> With that malignant cause wherein the honor
> Of my dear father's gift stands chief in power,
> I come to tender it and my appliance
> With all bound humbleness.
>
> (113–17)

After a short debate between himself and Helena, the king decides to give her a chance to cure him. She offers her life as the penalty should she fail; and as the reward for success:

> Then shalt thou give me with thy kingly hand
> With husband in thy power I will command.
>
> (198–99)

(Out of modesty, she of course excludes the royal bloodline of France.) The sickly king, amazed by this bold young woman, agrees, and then he asks to be helped from the stage:

> Unquestioned, welcome and undoubted blest.
> Give me some help here, ho! If thou proceed
> As high as word, my deed shall match thy deed.
>
> (211–13)

## Commentary

The framework of this scene provides insights into the two central characters, although Bertram and Helena are not seen together. There is something puppyish about Bertram; his feelings are hurt deeply because the rest of the young noblemen are riding off to battle while he must remain behind. Shakespeare paints a picture of youthful petulance and malleability in this part of the scene, as Parolles acts as a tempter and as a bad influence to Bertram. His advice is to ignore the king's command and, furthermore, to study the ways of the courtly gentlemen and soldiers in order to become a perfectly fashionable man of the world—presumably like Parolles himself. Of course, the audience (and virtually everyone else on stage besides Bertram) can see right through Parolles' bombast. One imagines the other noblemen urging Bertram and Parolles into their company with their tongues tucked firmly into their cheeks. Parolles typically stresses fashion (one wonders how outlandishly he is dressed) when talking to his companion: "Be more expressive to them, for they wear themselves in the cap of time; there do muster true gait, eat, speak, and move under the influence of the most received [up-to-date] star; and though the devil lead the measure, such are to be followed. After them, and take a more dilated [extended] farewell." The reference here to "devil" is Shakespeare's way of underlining a similarity in this situation to the "prodigal son" stories in the Bible and other traditional sources.

Consider Helena's behavior in the latter section of the scene. As a woman, she is conventionally conceived of as being frail; the thought of her being a professional (a doctor) is absurd; and the notion that she – a mere woman – could cure a *king* would normally be beyond imagining. Nevertheless, she overcomes the king's doubts, which are, given his time, reasonable enough. He fears that people will think that he's downright dotty if it were known that a "maiden" is attending him as a physician:

> I say we must not so stain our judgment or corrupt
>    our hope,
> To prostitute our past-cure malady to empirics
>    [quacks],
> Or to dissever so our great self and our credit,
> To esteem a senseless help, when help past sense we
>    deem.

> (122–25)

Using her skill of rhetoric, larded with aphoristic remarks like,

> Oft expectation fails, and most oft there
> Where most it promises, and oft it hits
> Where hope is coldest and despair most fits.

> (145–47)

Helena finally sways the king to give her a chance. Perhaps she nudges him over the edge by hinting that she is a divine emissary:

> But most it is presumption in us when
> The help of Heaven we count the act of men.
>
> (154–55)

Some critics have observed a trace of the fairy tale formula in this section of the play, in which the young virgin "magically" cures an ailing king. This may be so, but one cannot fail to be impressed by the sheer doggedness of Shakespeare's heroine. Her effort of will commands the end of the scene, contrasting with Bertram's jellyfish compliance at its opening.

# ACT II – SCENE 2

## Summary

The Countess and her clown/servant, Lavache, discourse on the subject of the "court," where he is shortly to be sent on an errand.

## Commentary

This comical interlude has a threefold function: (1) as a bridge, (2) as an emotional and thematic gloss on the scenes either side of it, and (3) as a simple entertainment in itself. Remember, Shakespeare's comic actors were given room for improvisation, and hence a scene like this one, obliquely satirizing courtly manners, could be largely visual in the person of the clown preparing himself to make an appearance before a group of courtiers. While practicing the art of foppishly affected speech – the inanely repeated "universal answer" to every question is "O Lord, sir!" – the clown is no doubt also training himself physically, in highly artificial, dance-like movements. *This,* Shakespeare seems to be saying, is the world to which Bertram wants to attach himself.

# ACT II – SCENE 3

## Summary

At first, Parolles, Bertram, and Lafeu are alone on stage, responding in awe to the healing of the king. Lafeu reads a report: "A showing of a heavenly effect in an earthly actor."

The king is quick to fulfill his promise, as he commands his noble-men to assemble before the triumphant healer, Helena:

> Thy frank election [choice] make;
> Thou hast power to choose, and they none to
> forsake . . .
> Who shuns thy love shuns all his love in me.

(61–62/79)

Helena tells all present that she has already made up her mind which man she'll have, but she nonetheless playfully approaches, and rejects, four others before coming to Bertram and saying,

> I dare not say I take you, but I give
> Me and my service, ever whilst I live,
> Into your guiding power. This is the man.

(109–11)

Bertram's shock at her choice prompts not only a feeling of rejection within Helena, but what amounts to an insult – "A poor physi-cian's daughter my wife! Disdain/ Rather corrupt me ever!" The king will have none of this, and he immediately lectures Bertram on the foolishness of social snobbery; then he exerts his power to command, forcing Bertram to take Helena's hand. Bertram submits, and the com-pany disperses.

Parolles denies his master to Lafeu,

> *Parolles:* Recantation! My lord! My master!
> *Lafeu:* Ay; is it not a language I speak?
> *Parolles:* A most harsh one, and not to be understood
> without bloody succeeding. My master!

(196–99)

And Lafeu, who admits having been impressed by the hanger-on, says,

I did think thee, for two ordinaries [meals],
To be a pretty wise fellow,

(211–12)

and then bids him good-riddance:

*Parolles:* My lord, you give me most egregious
indignity.
*Lafeu:* Ay, with all my heart, and thou art worthy
of it.

(228–29)

At Lafeu's exit, Bertram returns to Parolles with the words

O my Parolles, they have married me!
I'll to the Tuscan wars and never bed her.

(289–90)

Only too eager to escape a further confrontation with Lafeu and possible exposure as a false friend to Bertram, Parolles urges the younger man on "to other regions!"

## Commentary

The exposure of Parolles and the disgrace of Bertram accentuate this scene, one which otherwise would have depicted Helena's triumph. There is something unsettling in the atmosphere from the start, and even the curing of the king leaves little room overall for celebration, ending as it does in an outburst of anger by the healed party.

Shakespeare's dramaturgy works by continuously using contrasting scenes. Parolles' inane stuttering in Scene 3 – "So I say, so I say, So would I have said" – echoes the clown's mockery of "court" speech in Scene 2.

Contrast Helena's eloquence and wit in dealing with the assembled noblemen after, as she puts it, "Heaven hath through me restored the King to health." She typically snubs the First Lord with a quick rhyme: suit/mute.

> *Helena:* Now, Dian, from thy altar do I fly,
>   And to Imperial love, that god most high,
>   Do my sighs stream. [To First Lord:]
>   Sir, will you hear my suit?
> *First Lord:* And grant it.
> *Helena:* Thanks, sir, all the rest is mute.

(80–85)

Since Bertram has himself been mute through most of this scene, one wonders if it gradually dawns on him that Helena is preparing to choose him as her husband. In an earlier scene, she did say that "'Twas pretty, though a plague,/ To see him every hour, to sit and draw/ His arched brows, his hawking eye, his curls,/ In our heart's table." (I.1. 103–04). She apparently has spent hours watching him, perhaps not unnoticed. Still, there is a shock when the "sentence," as it seems to him, is pronounced:

> *King:* Why then, young Bertram, take her; she's thy
>   wife.
> *Bertram:* My wife, my liege! I shall beseech your
>   Highness,
>   In such business give me leave to use
>   The help of mine own eyes.
> *King:* Know'st thou not, Bertram,
>   What she has done for me?
> *Bertram:* Yes, my good lord;
>   But never hope to know why I should marry her.

(112–19)

Note that the king and the people in attendance on him were, according to the conventional pattern of social behavior in Shakespeare's day, undoubtedly shocked, and correctly so, at Bertram's refusal. Marriage was *not* considered primarily a romantic matter, though that of course played a part. The idea was that one could easily enough learn to love one's partner, and as the king clearly states, Helena's wealth and social station can be adjusted by his edict:

If thou canst like this creature as a maid,

> I can create the rest. Virtue and she
> Is her own dower; honor and wealth from me.
>
> (149–51)

Bertram's outburst is, to say the least, not very tactful in the presence of an old king and the lady who has restored the old king's life. Helena is embarrassed into saying, "Let the rest go [forget it]," when Bertram persists. There is a tremendous emotional awkwardness when the angry king insists on the marriage, saying that he "must produce [his] power" to secure his honor. Bertram's quick turnabout (a lie) and his exit with his "bride to be" must leave both the stage audience and the one in the theater feeling uneasy:

> I find that she, which late
> Was in my nobler thoughts most base, is now
> The praised of the King; who, so ennobled,
> Is as 'twere born so.
>
> (177–80)

This is especially so since Bertram and the doubly disgraced Parolles (who denied his master, then acted the coward toward old Lafeu) soon conspire to leave France and their obligations there for the wars in Italy where, ironically, Bertram expects to attain his "honour." As a final, sordid touch, Shakespeare has Bertram plan to send Helena back to Rousillon in possession of a sealed envelope addressed to the Countess, which will "acquaint my mother with my hate to her [Helena]."

## ACT II – SCENES 4 & 5

### Summary

Parolles interrupts Helena and the clown with a message from Bertram: Helena is to beg leave of the king, "strength'ned with what apology you think/ May make it probable need," and then to report back to Bertram. She "wait[s] upon his will."

In Scene 5, Lafeu tries to disillusion Bertram with regard to his false friend Parolles, but to little avail. Bertram: "I do assure you, my lord, he is very great in knowledge and accordingly valiant." Lafeu then openly insults Parolles to expose him: "There can be no kernel in this light nut; the soul of this man is his clothes." After Helena dutifully takes the letter which Bertram had planned to write in Scene 3 and is ready to go as commanded back to Rousillon, Bertram brushes her off, refusing to give her even a polite kiss in parting.

## Commentary

Even the clown mocks Parolles in this part of the play – "much fool may you find in you" – and Shakespeare makes it abundantly clear that either Bertram lacks all good judgment or else he is willfully behaving against the better advice of those around him in continuing his association with Parolles. Lafeu's departing words to Parolles, and Bertram's comment, perhaps indicate a slight second thought on the young man's part:

> *Lafeu:* Farewell, monsieur! I have spoken better of
> you
> Than you have or will to deserve at my hand,
> But we must do good against evil. *[Exit]*
> *Parolles:* An idle [stupid] lord, I swear.
> *Bertram:* I think so.
> *Parolles:* Why, do you not know him?
> *Bertram:* Yes, I do know him well, and common
> speech
> Gives him a worthy pass [reputation].
> (50–57)

Helena's arrival prevents this line of talk from going any further, however. Imagine the circumstances: Bertram, forced to take Helena's hand in marriage in full view of the assembled courtiers whose respect he craves, must now pretend at least a passing courtesy toward his "wife," even when in relative privacy. We know that he holds her in some contempt, and that the letter which he commands her to deliver viciously denounces her. She seems pathetic here, begging for Bertram's attention.

> *Bertram:* What would you have?

> *Helena:* Something, and scarce so much: nothing,
> indeed.
> I would not tell you what I would, my lord.
> Faith, yes!
> Strangers and foes do sunder and not kiss.
> *Bertram:* I pray you, stay not, but in haste to horse.
>
> (87–92)

Shakespeare doesn't say what Bertram does when Helena asks for a departing kiss, and one wonders what would be most effective: a half-hearted kiss, equivalent to a pat on the head, or a silence of two beats and an abruptly turned back?

# ACT III – SCENES 1 & 2

## Summary

In twenty-three lines, Shakespeare introduces the city of Florence, Italy, to the play while that city's Duke puzzles aloud to a French nobleman about the king of France's neutrality in the Italian wars. The French lord concurs: "Holy seems the quarrel/ Upon your Grace's part; black and fearful/ On the opposer."

In Scene 2, the clown has returned to Rousillon, where he delivers a letter from Bertram to his mother advising her that he has run away from his marriage; in the letter, he says: "If there be breadth enough in the world, I will hold a long distance." This upsets the Countess: "This is not well, rash and unbridled boy,/ To fly the favours of so good a King. . . ." Helena's distress, when she reads Bertram's letter to her, compounds the feeling. She labels his note a "passport"—that is, a license to beg on the open road—and says that it is a "dreadful sentence."

> When thou canst get the ring upon my finger,
> Which never shall come off, and show me a child
> Begotten of thy body that I am father to, then call
> Me husband; but in such a "then" I write a "Never."
>
> (59–62)

The Countess disavows Bertram as her son and then asks whether
or not he is still traveling in the company of Parolles, the "very tainted
fellow, and full of wickedness." The scene ends with a monologue
by Helena, who vows to leave France to clear the way for Bertram
to return home from the dangerous wars:

> No; come thou home, Rousillon,
> Whence honor but of danger wins a scar,
> As oft it loses all. I will be gone, –
> My being here it is that holds thee hence.
> Shall I stay here to do it? No, no.
>
> (123–27)

## Commentary

No doubt the clown has altered his appearance, somewhat, to be
like the fashionable set that he mingled with in Paris. His attitude
toward "mere provincials" has taken a radical turn too. Isbel was the
wench whom he begged permission to marry in Act I, but now,

> I have no mind to Isbel since I was at court.
> Our old lings [salt cod, slang for lechers] and our
> Isbels o' th' country are nothing like your
> Old lings, and your Isbels o' th' court.
>
> (13–16)

The Countess, for her part, responds to her "altered" son, young
Bertram. Note the number of times that he is referred to by her and
others as a "boy," implying immaturity. She cannot understand his
disobedience to the king in refusing to honor Helena, especially since
Helena is such a fine person. The Countess' words are meant to
assuage poor Helena's grief, but they seem harsh to her son:

> I prithee, lady, have a better cheer.
> If thou engrossest [take] all the griefs are thine,
> Thou robb'st me of a moiety [share]. He was my son,
> But I do wash his name out of my blood
> And thou art all my child.
>
> (67–71)

The "dreadful sentence" which Helena reads conjures up further associations with fairy tales and stories of legend. Here, one should remember the reference to the archetypal "curing of the king" story earlier in the play. Shakespeare uses a tradition in which a beleaguered bride must accomplish several "impossible" tasks, or overcome a number of severe trials in order to prove herself, and (usually) win the love of the man whom she loves. The plot elements in the rest of the play hinge on this "sentence," as Helena sets out to solve the riddle and overcome the obstacles which Bertram has set. She must get the ring from his finger (symbolic of family tradition and honor), and she must also become pregnant—despite Bertram's avowed dislike of her.

In a play which has far fewer passages of sheer poetic beauty than we have come to expect from Shakespeare, Helena's soliloquy here, expressing her torment, stands out even if it does use fairly commonplace metaphors:

> And is it I that drive thee from the sportive court,
> Where thou wast shot at with fair eyes,
> To be the mark of smoky muskets?
> O you leaden messengers,
> That ride upon the violent speed of fire,
> Fly with false aim, move the still-peering [self-repairing] air
> That sings with piercing; do not touch my lord!
>
> (111–17)

## ACT III – SCENES 3 & 4

### Summary

With the Duke's blessing, Bertram enters battle on behalf of the city state of Florence: "A lover of thy [Mars, god of War] drum, hater of love." In Rousillon, the Countess learns that Helena has left France, where she was a religious pilgrim; thus, she sends a letter via her steward to lure Bertram back:

> Write, write, Rinaldo, to this unworthy husband of his wife;

Let every word lay heavy of her worth that he does
    weigh too light.
My greatest grief, though little he do feel it, set down
    sharply.
Dispatch the most convenient messenger.
When haply he shall hear that she is gone,
He will return.

(29–34)

## Commentary

Helena's dismay and Bertram's eagerness to be an honorable
soldier contrast sharply in these short scenes. Note that as the play
moves along, more and more people are becoming embroiled in decep-
tive schemes. Now the Countess hopes to lure her son back with the
news that Helena is out of the country. She is sure that Helena will
then come back, "led hither by pure love."

# ACT III – SCENE 5

## Summary

The "old Widow of Florence," her daughter Diana, and a girl
named Mariana, a "neighbor to the Widow," talk about the brave
exploits of the "French Count" (Bertram), and about his wooing of
Diana (through his intermediary, the "filthy officer" Parolles). Mariana
warns Diana of Bertram's and Parolles' trickery ("engines of lust"), and
at that moment, Helena arrives, "disguised as a [religious] pilgrim."
After exchanging pleasantries and establishing that Helena will stay
overnight in the widow's house, the women turn their attention to
the triumphantly returning Count Bertram. Diana says,

He stole from France, as 'tis reported,
For the King had married him against his liking.

(55–56)

Helena further learns that the Count's follower Parolles "reports coarse-
ly" of Bertram's wife, and with irony, she sadly says of the "wife"
(herself): "She is too mean [common] to have her name repeated." The
Count arrives, and he briefly luxuriates in his glorious return, and

then the women go to the widow's, where Helena has invited all of them to dinner at her expense.

## Commentary

Shakespeare was no geographer. He has Helena on her way to a shrine in Santiago de Compostela, Spain, by way of Florence, although Helena started out in southern France. But no matter. The dramatic point is that Helena, who has humbled herself for the sake of her love, further associates herself with "heaven" by adopting the guise of a pilgrim, and is now about to reach a low point in her personal anguish before reversing the order of things. She stresses her own unworthiness while learning of the Count's lascivious pursuit of other women. When she asks about Bertram's interest in Diana, one wonders whether a plan to ensnare him is hatching itself in her brain:

> *Widow:* This young maid might do her a shrewd turn
> [help her out].
> *Helena:* How do you mean? Maybe the amorous
> Count
> Solicits her in the unlawful purpose.
> *Widow:* He does indeed, and brokes [deals]
> With all that can in such a suit
> Corrupt the tender honour of a maid.
>
> (69–74)

When Bertram actually appears with "drum and colors," Helena pretends not to know who he is. "Which is the Frenchman?" she asks. Perhaps she wants to give Diana the opportunity to betray any secret romantic longing which she might have for him. Diana's tone of voice, if not her words, would be sure to give her away. Apparently, Helena is satisfied that no such attraction exists, for she soon solicits Diana's aid in trapping Bertram.

## ACT III – SCENES 6 & 7

### Summary

Several French lords prevail upon Bertram to let them prove that

Parolles is a scoundrel unworthy of his company. They will set Parolles up to recapture a drum which he lost in battle (a military disgrace), then they will capture and blindfold him, and in Bertram's presence, they will get him to "betray you [Bertram] and deliver all the intelligence in his power against you." Bertram agrees to the plot. Parolles enters and takes the bait:

> *Parolles:* I know not what the success will be,
> My lord, but the attempt I vow.
> *Bertram:* I know, thou'rt valiant; and to the
> Possibility of thy soldiership will subscribe
> For thee. Farewell.
> *Parolles:* I love not many words. *[Exit]*
> *First Lord:* No more than fish loves water.
> Is not this a strange fellow, my lord,
> That so confidently seems to undertake this
> Business, which he knows is not to be done,
> Damns himself to do, and dares better be
> Damned than to do it?
>
> (86–97)

Bertram ends Scene 6 asking a lord to intercede for him to "the lass I spoke of" (Diana).

Helena, for her part, bribes the Widow of Florence to help her convince Diana to allow herself to be used as a decoy in trapping Bertram. Helena wants Diana to, first, get the Count's ring in exchange for the promise of future favors, and then to set up an "encounter" with him.

> In fine, delivers me to fill the time,
> Herself most chastely absent. After,
> To marry her [pay her dowry] I'll add three thousand
> crowns
> To what is past already.
>
> (33–36)

## Commentary

A "noble" Count (Bertram) agrees to entrap a friend, and a "chaste" maiden (Helena) offers large sums of money to a mother to get her daughter to arrange to have sexual intercourse with a legally married man. The plot now grows murky in this unusual "comedy." As Parolles is himself dishonest, however, there is a kind of justice in ensnaring him: the trickster will himself be tricked. Yet Bertram himself (like Parolles) seems disloyal. A similar parallel exists in Shakespeare's *Henry IV, Part 1*, in which Hal's delightful scoundrel-companion, fat Jack Falstaff, is exposed publicly as a coward for the good of young Prince Hal. The difference, of course, is that Hal has known all along what mettle Falstaff is made of, and Hal himself is of enormously greater stature than Bertram. Bertram is petty by comparison, as is this scheme to expose and tease the loathsome Parolles.

Helena's plan also has a darker element, for she does have the matter of "right" on her side:

> *Helena:* Why then tonight let us essay our plot,
>   Which, if it speed, is wicked meaning [Bertram's]
>   In a lawful deed, and lawful meaning
>   In a lawful act [Helena's]
>   Where both not sin, and yet a sinful fact.
>   But let's about it.
>
> (43–48)

Helena undertakes the adventure with relish, and she paves the way with purses of gold to the Widow of Florence and her virgin daughter, Diana. The quoted passage captures all the ambiguity of the plot – Bertram will be making love to Helena, his rightful wife, though he thinks that she is Diana, an attractive virgin whom he fancies. His *intention* will be sinful, although the *act* will be lawful. "Ethics be damned!" seems to be Helena's attitude, so long as "all ends well" and is just.

## ACT IV – SCENE 1

### Summary

One of the French lords and a band of soldiers set a trap for Parolles as previously planned. They capture and blindfold him and speak in a hilarious nonsense language which he takes to be Russian – that is, *"Throca movousus, cargo, cargo, cargo."* To save his life, Parolles, as predicted, immediately volunteers to betray anyone and anything:

Oh, let me live!
And all the secrets of our camp I'll show,
Their force, their purposes; nay, I'll speak that
Which you will wonder at.

(92–95)

*Commentary*

For Parolles, the Falstaffian mock-motto, "Discretion is the better part of valor," seems to apply. There is no real surprise in his behavior, although his captors marvel at his self-knowledge:

> *Parolles:* What shall I say I have done? It must be a very
> Plausive [plausible] invention that carries it.
> They begin to smoke me [find me out], and disgraces
> Have of late knocked too often at my door. I find
> My tongue is too foolhardy.
> *First Lord [aside]:* This is the first truth that e'er thine own
> Tongue was guilty of.
> *Second Lord:* Is it possible he should know what he is, and
> Be that he is?
>
> (28–36)

There is a sly joke embedded in this scene, in which the "man of words" (which is what Parolles' *name* literally means) is tricked by a plot which makes use of some assorted syllables of a gobbledygook language that Parolles thinks is Russian.

# ACT IV – SCENE 2

**Summary**

Bertram woos the widow's daughter, Diana, with success, or so he thinks, and therefore, he gives her his family ring as a token of their arranged meeting:

>*Bertram:* It is an honour, 'longing to our house,
>Bequeathed down from many ancestors,
>Which were the greatest obloquy i' th' world
>In me to lose.
>*Diana:* Mine honour's such a ring;
>My chastity's the jewel of our house,
>Bequeathed down from many ancestors,
>Which were the greatest obloquy i' th' world
>In me to lose.
>
>(42–50)

Diana agrees to let Bertram into her chamber at midnight on condition that he remain absolutely silent during their encounter and that they stay together for one hour only. At that time, she will place another ring on his finger, "that what [which] in time proceeds/ May token to the future our past deeds."

## Commentary

The language in this scene is bland – Bertram utters cliches, calculated to capture the fancy of a girl with whom he wants to have sex, and she knows it:

>My mother told me just how he would woo,
>As if she sat in 's heart. She says all men
>Have the like oaths.
>
>(67–69)

Diana is, of course, acting for a price, yet notice the delight she takes in teasing Bertram along the way. He tells her, Parolles-like, that her cold manner is inappropriate, that she should be "as your mother was/ When your sweet self was got." Diana's reply is calculated to irritate:

>*Diana:* No. My mother did but duty;
>Such my lord, as you owe to your wife.
>*Bertram:* No more o' that!
>
>(12–14)

Shakespeare drives the point home that Bertram is very irresponsible when he relinquishes his family ring; Diana mockingly repeats, word for word, his "bequeathed down from many ancestors" speech.

## ACT IV – SCENE 3

**Summary**

Two French lords, the brothers Dumain, discuss Bertram's situation briefly before he enters to witness their exposure of Parolles. They are aware of Bertram's improprieties, including the deception of Helena (whom they presume to be dead, as rumor has it) and the "perversion" of Diana, "a young gentlewoman here in Florence, of a most chaste renown." They are certain that his current glory will do no good when he returns to France: "The great dignity that his valour hath here acquired for him shall at home be encount'red with a shame as ample."

Bertram swaggers before his countrymen as he enters: "I have congied with [taken leave of] the Duke, done my adieu with his nearest, buried a wife, mourned for her, writ to my lady mother I am returning, entertained my convoy, and between these main parcels of dispatch effected many nicer needs; the last was the greatest, but that I have not ended yet."

The bulk of the scene is taken up with Parolles' exposure and disgrace. Brought in blindfolded and pricked on with the merest hint of physical torture, he reveals military secrets (probably made-up), slanders Bertram and the brothers Dumain, and shows himself to be an utterly craven liar and a cheat. Bertram had thought of him as a confidant, yet the letter which Parolles planned to give Diana reads:

> Men are to mell with, boys are not to kiss:
> For count of this, the Count's a fool, I know it,
> Who pays before, but not when he does owe it.

> (257–59)

When his life seems threatened, Parolles' hypocrisy is at its greatest:

> My life, sir, in any case! Not that I
> Am afraid to die, but that my offenses

> Being many I would repent out the remainder of
>    nature.
> Let me live, sir, in a dungeon, i' th' stocks,
> Or anywhere, so I may live.

(270–74)

Bertram and the others squeeze as much villainy from him as they can before removing his hood, whereupon, speechless he must face them. When they leave, he shrugs a remark to one of the soldiers, "Who cannot be crushed with a plot?"

## Commentary

Parolles is what he is! Small consolation when the subject is so mean-spirited, yet Shakespeare in this scene almost seems to place the "gallant knave" in positive contrast against his master, Bertram. Dumain marvels at the extent of Parolles' corruption. It is clear to the French lord that this man is embroidering falsehoods in order to save his skin, and it becomes enjoyable to witness.

> *Parolles* [of the French Lord]: I have but little more
>        to say,
>    Sir, of his honesty – he has everything that an
>    Honest man should not have; what an honest
>        man
>    Should have, he has nothing.
> *First Lord* [aside]: I begin to love him for this.
> *Bertram* [aside]: For this description of thine honesty?
>    A pox upon him for me, he's more and more a
>        cat.

(287–93)

The First Lord, enjoying the exposure of Parolles, seems to confirm the feeling that the culprit expresses at the very end of the scene: "There's place and means for every man alive."

# ACT IV – SCENES 4 & 5

## Summary

Helena assures the widow and Diana that their help will be rewarded: ". . . Heaven/ Hath brought me up to be your daughter's dower." In other words, they will simply have to endure a bit longer until the plot reaches its end.

In Rousillon, Lafeu comforts the Countess, who believes that Helena has died, "the most virtuous gentlewoman that ever Nature had praise for creating." They discuss the return of Bertram and the anticipated arrival of the King of France, who "comes post [haste] from Marseilles, of as able body as when he numbered thirty [was thirty years old]." A match is proposed between Lafeu's daughter and Bertram. Also present is the clown Lavache, whose wordplay and sexual jokes grow tedious to Lafeu.

### Commentary

Things grow worse before they get better, although "all's well that ends well," as Helena assures Diana. The scene at Rousillon is out of joint, and even the clown "has no face, but runs where he will." The "death" of Helena weighs on their minds, and the clown's off-color foolery seems grating and very much out of place, even to the point where Lafeu "grows aweary" of him. The clown remarks on a scar which Bertram is covering with "a patch of velvet." Such a scar might be the result of an honorable encounter in battle, yet to Lavache it seems more likely to be the mark of a lanced ulcer, of the sort which appears on syphilitics. This ugly note closes the scene.

## ACT V – SCENES 1 & 2

### Summary

Helena, the widow and Diana are in pursuit of the king, whom they know to have traveled to Marseilles. Once there, they learn from a gentleman that the king has left in haste for Rousillon. Helena asks him to speed ahead with a message for the king.

In Rousillon, Parolles is begging the clown to deliver a letter of his own to Lafeu, when that gentleman appears. After teasing Parolles about his fallen status, Lafeu shows pity and bids Parolles to follow him to the count's palace (where the king has arrived), saying, "Though you are a fool and a knave, you shall eat."

## Commentary

Noteworthy here is the clown's relish in teasing Parolles with numerous scatalogical references to the "stench" he finds himself in with Fortune and society – "Fortune's close-stool" [toilet] and "a purn [dung] of Fortune" – and Lafeu's contrasting good-humored forgiveness of the knavish fellow.

# ACT V – SCENE 3

## Summary

The Countess begs the king to forgive her son, which he does at once, and he also confirms a match between Lafeu's daughter (Maudlin) and Bertram. Bertram is quick to accept the king's suggestion of a bride *this* time:

> *King:* You remember the daughter of this lord?
> *Bertram:* Admiringly, my liege. At first
> I stuck my choice upon her, ere my heart
> Durst make too bold a herald of my tongue.
>
> (43–46)

He gives Lafeu a ring as token of his pledge, and the old gentleman recognizes it immediately:

> Helen, that's dead, was a sweet creature;
> Such a ring as this,
> The last that e'er I took her leave at court,
> I saw upon her finger.
>
> (74–77)

To make matters worse for Bertram, the king now recognizes the ring as the one which he gave to Helena as a "token" by which she could summon help if she ever needed it. Furthermore, the king says,

> She [Helena] called the saints to surety
> That she would never put it from her finger,
> Unless she gave it to yourself in bed.
>
> (108–10)

Bertram is taken away. Helena's messenger then enters with a letter claiming to be from Diana, which sues for her right to be Bertram's wife: "Otherwise a seducer flourishes and a poor maid is undone."

Diana confronts Bertram, then Parolles is brought in to testify as to the details of Bertram's behavior. The king nearly reaches the point of exasperation with Diana's cryptic half-explanations of what actually went on: "She does abuse our ears. To prison with her!" Then Helena reveals herself, at which sight the king says:

> Is there no exorcist
> Beguiles the truer office of mine eyes?
> Is't real that I see?
>
> (305–07)

The play quickly resolves itself, with Helena and Bertram together and Diana promised a dowry. "All yet seems well, and if it end so meet," says the king, "The bitter past, more welcome is the sweet."

## Commentary

So much transpires so quickly in this scene that it threatens to "run away with the play," turning it into a romp and a farce. Consider the hero, who has apparently returned home as a respected (penitent) nobleman, fresh from the Florentine wars. The king forgives him, as does his mother, for his disobedience and his disgraceful behavior toward Helena, whom they describe in hushed tones fitting for a saint. Ready to accept the king's second offer of a bride (Lafeu's daughter) and thus secure his position in Rousillon, the world suddenly turns upside down for him. The king recognizes his ring, and all accuse Bertram of foul play in Helena's demise: "I am wrapped in dismal thinkings," comments the king. Furthermore, Diana appears, demanding her rights as Bertram's "lawful bride." Before Helena appears to clarify the situation, Bertram undergoes a painful series of embarrassments, all the more troubling to him because he had opened the scene in full command of his new life. Now, he is forced into a situation in which his lies are openly revealed, even before the weasel Parolles—his "equivocal companion."

In the language of riddles, Diana prepares the way for the sudden re-reversal:

He knows himself my bed he hath defiled,
And at that time, he got his wife with child.
Dead though she be, she feels her young one kick.
So, there's my riddle: one that's dead is quick
        [both alive *and* pregnant].
            (301–04)

When Helena walks onstage, resurrected from the "dead" and pregnant with a new "life," the king (and presumably everyone else present except Diana) stands aghast. Thus it is that he calls for an exorcist. The comedy has run its course from opening gloom to "miraculous" joy. Between here and the end of the play, barely thirty-five lines transpire, hardly time for reflection. There is also something tentative (and comical) in this love-pledge by Count Bertram of Rousillon:

If she, my liege, can make me know this clearly
    [that is, all that has transpired],
I'll love her dearly, ever, ever dearly.
            (316–17)

Ironically, one wonders, finally, just how "well" all this has really ended.

## QUESTIONS FOR REVIEW

1. Why does Bertram refuse to marry Helena?

2. How is it possible that Helena is able to cure the King of France of his malady?

3. Why is Parolles considered to be a poor companion for Bertram?

4. What are the two "tasks" that Helena must accomplish before Bertram is willing to recognize her as his wife?

5. How does the ring of the King of France figure into the plot?

6. For whom does Helena weep early in the play?

7. Comment on the effect of the "gloomy mood" during the first scene of this play.

8. What role does "honor" play in the lives of Helena, Bertram, Parolles, the King of France, and Diana?

9. There is a good deal of sexual wordplay in the comedy; what are the reactions of Helena and the Countess?

10. Characterize the Countess' attitude toward Bertram.

11. Why is the guise of a religious pilgrim especially apt for Helena?

12. Explain the "resurrection theme" in this play.

# THE MERRY WIVES OF WINDSOR

## INTRODUCTION

There are three early texts of *Merry Wives;* the first two (printed in the First Quarto and the Second Quarto) are garbled and are only half as long as the version printed in what we have come to believe is the authoritative version – that is, the version in the First Folio. Seemingly, however, even the First Folio edition is incomplete, for there are non sequiturs in the play, referring to a horse-stealing episode and a deer-poaching episode which are not developed. Furthermore, it is believed that the First Folio version was taken from a script that belonged to the man playing the Host of the Garter Inn. Only his lines are fully developed. The rest of the play is largely filled with paraphrases and mangled lines.

Critics also tend to believe an eighteenth-century writer who refers to this play as having been commissioned by Queen Elizabeth herself. "It [*Merry Wives*] had pleased one of the greatest Queens that ever was in the World," he writes, adding that "this Comedy was written at her Command . . . and she commanded it to be finished in fourteen days." Another eighteenth-century scholar mentions that Elizabeth was "so well pleas'd with that admirable Character of *Falstaff,* in the two parts of *Henry the Fourth,* that she commanded him to continue it for one Play more, and to shew him in Love." This deadline, of course, could explain the sloppy attention to plot and subplot lines.

Scholars have also said that the verse in *Merry Wives* is so poor that the comedy *sounds* un-Shakespearean. But they laud the creation yet again of the Falstaff character. He is a glorious figure of fun. And the "wives" are indeed "merry," and even the jealous Ford is changed into a man of merriment when the play finally ends.

## BRIEF PLOT SUMMARY

*The Merry Wives of Windsor* is the most purely farcical of all of

Shakespeare's plays. It depends on lightning-quick timing between the actors and the carefully choreographed actions. The "meaning" cannot be separated from the "performance."

The incidents themselves are as follows: There is a main plot in which Sir John Falstaff conspires to seduce Mrs. Page and Mrs. Ford, the wives of two prominent Windsor citizens. The women play along with him in order to expose him as a preposterous lecher. Then, to complicate matters, the insanely jealous Mr. Ford disguises himself as one "Mr. Brook" and hires Falstaff to procure Mrs. Ford for him in order to (so he plans) reveal her suspected infidelity. But Mrs. Ford and Mrs. Page dupe both Falstaff *and* Mr. Ford. On one occasion, Falstaff is tricked into hiding in a basket of dirty clothes, then dropped into the river ("I have a kind of alacrity in sinking," he says); on another occasion, he must disguise himself as a fat old woman, a "witch" much hated by Mr. Ford, who summarily pummels "her"/him. Finally, both husbands join their "merry wives" in an elaborate masque-like entertainment, the high point of which is the humiliation of Falstaff, who has this time disguised himself as the ghostly "Herne the Hunter," complete with a massive set of horns on his head.

The secondary plot concerns the comical antics of a pair of would-be suitors for the hand of the lovely Anne Page. Doctor Caius, a quick-tempered French doctor, and Slender, the stupid nephew of Justice Shallow, vie for Anne's favor, while she finds both of them abhorrent. Sir Hugh Evans, a friend to Shallow and a supporter of Slender's cause, comes into conflict with Doctor Caius, and because the *Welshman* Evans and the *Frenchman* Caius persistently garble the English language, their meetings and arguments give special pleasure to all present.

In the end, Anne Page marries her true-love, a poor young gentleman named Fenton. Mr. Ford promises to desist from being jealous of his wife, Falstaff is made a laughing stock, and then he is reconciled to the group. The spirit of the comedy is best summed up in Mrs. Page's last lines:

> Master Fenton
> Heaven give you many, many merry days!
> Good husband, let us every one go home,
> And laugh this sport o'er by a country fire;
> Sir John and all.
>
> (253–57)

# LIST OF CHARACTERS

## Sir John Falstaff

Consistent with the image of the ne'er-do-well companion of
Prince Hal (later to be Henry V) in several of Shakespeare's history
plays, the Falstaff of *The Merry Wives of Windsor* is self-consciously
pompous and eloquent, self-pitying when the occasion arises, and
always ready to exploit anyone – man or woman – to achieve his de-
sired ends. His appetites and his humor are as large as his enormous
belly, and it is fitting that when he makes a fool of himself, as he
does no less than three times in this play, his folly looms larger than
that of the rest of the company combined. In order to secure his financial position and also to indulge his sexual fancy, he makes romantic
overtures to the "merry wives" of Windsor, Mrs. Page and Mrs. Ford.
They dupe him again and again: first, they stuff him into a "buck-
basket" full of ill-smelling linens and then have him dumped into the
Thames River; then, they disguise him as the fat "witch of Brainford,"
who is hated by Mr. Ford, who beats him black and blue; and finally,
they trick him into playing the part of "Herne the Hunter," a ghost
who haunts Windsor Park with great ragged horns on his head. In
the last disguise, Falstaff is surprised by the entire company and is
made the butt of their jokes. He admits to being "made an ass" in the
very last scene and is welcomed to join the group to "laugh this sport
o'er by a country fire."

## Fenton, a Young Gentleman

Master Fenton is the well-born but impecunious rightful lover in
this romantic farce. He successfully pursues young Anne Page over
the objections of both her mother and her father. The play ends fit-
tingly just after he announces their secret wedding. His bride has
married him in defiance of her parents, he says, "to shun/ A thou-
sand irreligious cursed hours/ Which forced marriage would have
brought upon her."

## Shallow, a Country Justice

Shallow's main part in the action, aside from swearing to be
revenged on Falstaff, is to propose and encourage the courtship of
Anne Page by his nephew, Slender.

## Slender, Nephew to Shallow

Slender's name describes his wit. He is one of Anne Page's unlikely suitors, a man possessing "a little wee face, with a little yellow beard," who prefers talking sport (dogs, bears, and "jests with geese") to courting women. At his uncle's insistence, he makes several romantic overtures to Anne, deluding even himself into thinking that he's in love with her, before the whole enterprise founders.

## Ford, a Citizen of Windsor ("Brook," in disguise)

Ford is a man of property who can be "mad as a mad dog" when jealousy overtakes him. Disguised as Brook, he pays Falstaff handsomely to compromise "Ford's" wife, but on both occasions, Mrs. Ford has the laugh on both Falstaff and on her husband. In the end, Ford admits his folly ("Pardon me, wife") and joins her in humiliating Falstaff in the final Herne-the-Hunter episode.

## Page, a Citizen of Windsor

Page is more reasonable than his friend Ford in every respect but one. Though he can see through his friend's jealousy, he cannot see the folly in his own choice of a husband for his daughter Anne. Refusing to consider Fenton as a possibility because Fenton has no property or money, Page favors Slender. His values are stolidly middle class; but for Shakespeare, who came from the same middle class himself, Page's good sense finally prevails over his property instincts, and he consents (after the fact) to the wedding of Anne and Fenton.

## William Page, the young son of Page

William appears in two scenes: first, he is doing his Latin lessons before Hugh Evans and Mistress Quickly; and second, he acts as one of the forest creatures in the elaborate ritual to unmask Falstaff in Windsor Park.

## Sir Hugh Evans, a Welsh Parson

Falstaff aptly hits on the most interesting feature of this character when he says that Evans "makes fritters of English." This remark is in response to Sir Hugh's line, typically in dialect: "Seese is not goot to give putter. Your pelly is all putter.": (Cheese is not good to give butter; your belly is all butter.)

## Doctor Caius, a French Physician

Another practitioner of fractured English (e.g., "If dere be one, or two, I shall make a de turd" ["third"]), Doctor Caius is Hugh Evans' chief antagonist. A revenger's subplot ensues when Caius learns that Hugh Evans is aiding Slender and Shallow in pursuit of Anne Page, a woman whom Caius himself fancies. Engineered by the Host of the Garter, a duel between these two is set to take place – in *different* locations. The Host, and the audience, would rather hear them argue than see them fight anyway. As retribution, Evans and Caius plan to seek joint revenge on the Host for this trick, and vague reference is made in the play to horses which they *may* have arranged to have stolen from the Host.

## The Host of the Garter Inn

The Host's chief motivation seems to be to enjoy himself. He babbles endlessly to all around him while engineering such schemes as the abortive duel between Doctor Caius and Sir Hugh Evans. This trickster, however, finds himself tricked too by the end of the play.

## Bardolph, Pistol, and Nym; followers of Falstaff

This crew of motley thieves, familiar from the other "Falstaff plays," has only a small part in the action here. They form a rogues' context for Falstaff. Their attitudes toward one another seem to be ones of mutual contempt, for they betray each other at every turn. Nym seems to utter the word "humour" in every sentence which he speaks; Bardolph becomes quickly familiar to us because of his references to his bulbous nose and his scarlet complexion; and Pistol stands out as the most venomous of Falstaff's inner circle of "friends."

## Simple, Servant to Slender

Even stupider than his master, Simple is usually the yo-yo of other people's witticisms.

## Mistress Ford

Reasonably cautious at first, Mrs. Ford soon decides not only to teach Falstaff a lesson for his outrageous presumption in trying to seduce her, but also to irritate her jealous husband and to expose his foolishness. At the end of the play, this "merry wife" reaffirms her marriage on the basis of trust, thereby creating a second reason for celebrating Fenton and Anne Page's nuptials.

## Mistress Page

Mrs. Page has the luxury of material comfort, a trusting husband, and lovely children. Hers is the advantage of the Elizabethan middle class. Her sense of morality is outraged by fat John Falstaff's proposals, and she sets out with her partner, Mrs. Ford, to expose Falstaff as a lecher and a fraud. This done, her (and her class') morality is re-affirmed. Yet Mrs. Page has a blind spot: she prefers the advantages which highly placed social connections can give her and believes that her daughter, Anne Page, should marry Doctor Caius. Anne's opinion of the Frenchman is clear: "I had rather be set quick i' th' earth,/ And bowled to death with turnips." The audience, of course, concurs and is happy that Mrs. Page can finally see the rightness of her daughter's marriage to Fenton.

## Anne Page

Anne is the model of "pretty virginity," the conventional beautiful maiden at the core of a romantic comedy. She adds her mother's pluck and forthrightness to her physical attributes, resists her parents' choice of suitors, and finally has her way with her male counterpart, Fenton.

## Mistress Quickly

Mistress Quickly, the talkative and meddlesome servant of Doctor Caius, uses her intimate friendship with Anne Page to turn a profit. She promotes all comers who think they have a hope of successfully wooing Anne Page. Quickly is as apt to misuse the English language as the Frenchman or Welshman are in the play, and she also provides some comedy in her penchant for obscene puns. It is especially amusing that she should play the part of the delicate Fairy Queen in the climactic "masque scene."

# SUMMARIES AND COMMENTARIES

## ACT I – SCENE 1

**Summary**

The "Country Justice" Shallow complains to Sir Hugh Evans, a Welsh parson, about a wrong which has been done to him by Sir John Falstaff: "I will make a Star-Chamber matter of it. If he were twenty Sir John Falstaffs, he shall not abuse Robert Shallow, Esquire." Sir Hugh momentarily calms the angry waters by suggesting a profitable scheme involving Shallow's nephew, Slender, who is also present. He suggests a "marriage between Master Abraham [Slender] and Mistress Anne Page," the beautiful and soon-to-be-wealthy daughter of a prominent "citizen of Windsor." Slender, the would-be wooer, thinks that he knows her: "She has brown hair and speaks small like a woman?"

The three then make plans to go to Page's house, where Falstaff is said to be. After exchanging greetings with Page, Shallow faces the wrongdoer himself:

> *Falstaff:* Now, Master Shallow, you'll complain of me
>   to the King?
> *Shallow:* Knight, you have beaten my man, killed my
>   deer, and broke open my lodge.
> *Falstaff:* But not kissed your keeper's daughter?
> *Shallow:* Tut, a pin [a trifle]! This shall be answered.
> *Falstaff:* I will answer it straight. I have done all this.
>   That is now answered.
>
> (112–18)

Slender adds his complaint against Falstaff's "cony-catching" rascal-friends, Bardolph, Nym, and Pistol. "They carried me to the tavern and made me drunk, and afterward picked my pocket. Egged on by their ringleader, Falstaff, the three "rascals" make elaborate denials of any questionable behavior.

Mistress Ford, Mistress Page, and Anne Page enter and, together with the rest of the company, are bid by Miss Page to come to "have a hot venison pasty to dinner." Sir Hugh and Shallow prevail upon Slender to pursue Anne Page. "I will marry her, sir, at your request;

but if there be no great love in the beginning, yet heaven may decrease it upon better acquaintance when we are married and have more occasion to know one another. I hope, upon familiarity will grow more content." The scene ends with a conversation between Anne and Slender about "why" he cannot join them in dinner. Eventually, however, Page persuades him to do so.

## Commentary

The first words of the play introduce its main figure by name – Sir John Falstaff. Though Justice Shallow's complaint against Falstaff (deer trapping) is completely forgotten once the main action gets underway, Shakespeare's choice to open the play in this way is dramatically effective. For Shakespeare's contemporary audience – and for anyone today who is familiar with his *Henry IV* plays – a mere reference to the comical misdeeds of the "huge hill of flesh," as Prince Hal (in *Henry IV*) refers to Falstaff, would whet the appetite. The buzz of anger which consumes Shallow conjures up memories of Falstaff's past chicanery and the irritation it has caused, especially to "right-thinking" citizens in other plays. Falstaff's first appearance in *Merry Wives*, pompous and full of disdain for others, is eminently enjoyable. In response to Shallow's bluster of accusation, Falstaff chooses to be tight-lipped: "I will answer it straight. . . . That is now answered." In other words, "I did it. So what?"

From the start, this comedy is different from Shakespeare's other comedies. It is his only completely "English" comedy, set in Windsor, and dealing with distinctly contemporary types. The language has the highest percentage of prose of all of Shakespeare's plays, indicating an attention to the "everyday" aspect and a focus on comic situations rather than to style.

The comic types in the first scene are broadly sketched. Sir Hugh Evans, the Welshman, is fond of displaying his learning, and he speaks in dialect, much to Falstaff's (and the audience's) amusement:

> *Evans: Pauca verba* [few words], Sir John; goot worts [good words].
> *Falstaff:* Good worts [cabbage]! Good cabbage.
> Slender, I broke your head.
> (123–25)

Shallow is eager to match his rather slow-witted nephew to Anne Page because there is money to be made in the deal ["seven hundred pounds and possibilities"]. The issues of money, morality, and marriage, then, are at the core of this farce. Slender, only vaguely aware of the money issue, is a monument of foolishness. His real joy is talking about dogs (to Page) and bears (to Anne), which makes him a comical suitor for the hand of the beautiful and gracious Mistress Page. Their scenes together offer some of the funniest moments in the play.

## ACT I – SCENES 2 & 3

### Summary

Evans sends Slender's servant, Simple, with a message to Mistress Quickly "to desire and require her to solicit your master's desires to Mistress Anne Page."

Falstaff, meanwhile, conspires with his men at the Garter Inn to "make love to Ford's wife" because "the report goes she has all the rule of her husband's purse." He sends Nym and Pistol with love letters to Mistress Page *and* to Mistress Ford, then exits. With Falstaff out of the room, his confederates prepare to betray him:

> *Nym:* I will discuss the humour of his love to Page
> [Mistress Page's husband].
> *Pistol:* And I to Ford shall eke unfold
> How Falstaff, varlet vile,
> His dove will prove, his gold will hold,
> And his soft couch defile.
>
> (104–08)

### Commentary

Falstaff is a knight "almost out at heels," and therefore, he sees as his natural prey the well-off middle class. Since he fancies himself a lover – "Page's wife . . . gave me good eyes too" – it is this talent which he will exploit to make money. The language which he uses to describe the woman whom he plans to woo is replete with references to the great age of the English merchant-adventurers:

She bears the purse too. She is a region in Guiana,
all gold and bounty. I will be cheaters [both financial Warder and "cheat," in the modern sense] to them
both, and they shall be exchequers to me. They shall
be my East and West Indies, and I will trade to them
both.

(75–79)

To see this "cheater" cheated – that is, Falstaff – will be one of the chief
pleasures in the play, and Pistol and Nym's quick decision to betray
their captain anticipates the fun.

# ACT I – SCENE 4

## Summary

Simple describes his master to Mistress Quickly, to whom he has
gone at Hugh Evans' bidding:

He hath but a little wee face, with a little yellow
beard – a Cain-coloured [red] beard.

(22–23)

Quickly agrees to help Shallow in his plans to woo Anne Page, but
before she can elaborate, her own master, the "French physician"
Doctor Caius, returns home. Simple is shuffled into a "closet," or a
small side room, just seconds before Caius enters. The doctor plans
to go to the "court," taking his servant John Rugby with him. He dis-
covers Simple and is outraged to learn that the latter is on an errand
to curry favor with Anne Page through the agency of Mistress Quickly.
Since Caius wants the young lady for himself, he immediately writes
a letter of challenge to Sir Hugh and sends it with Simple. The last
of the suitors then arrives, a "young gentleman" by the name of Fenton.
Quickly assures him that he too will continue his courtship of Anne
Page.

*Quickly:* Have not your worship a wart above your
eye?
*Fenton:* Yes, marry, have I. What of that?

> *Quickly:* Well, thereby hangs a tale. Good faith, it is
> such another Nan [girl]; but, I detest, an honest
> maid as ever broke bread. We had an hour's talk
> of that wart.
>
> (156–60)

Fenton gives her money for her efforts and exits, whereupon she admits (to the audience) that "Anne loves him not."

## Commentary

Shakespeare expands his gallery of odd characters in this scene – Rugby, whose "worst fault is that he is given to prayer"; Quickly, who is ready to please anyone as a go-between if the price is right, and who fractures the English language every time she opens her mouth ("but, I detest, an honest maid," etc.); and finally, the irascible French doctor and would-be lover, Caius. One of the few more or less "normal" characters in the play, Fenton has a "wart above his eye."

The pacing of this play must be *very* fast or the farce will not be effective. In the first moments of this short scene, there is a concealment and a near-discovery (Caius first sends Quickly to fetch his "green box" from the "closet" where Simple is hiding), which makes the discovery which follows all the more comical. The joke is compounded by Doctor Caius' unintentional pun when he returns to the "closet" himself:

> Dere is some simples in my closset dat I vill not
> Vor de varld I shall leave behind.
>
> (65–66)

Caius means "medicines" by the word "simples," but Quickly and Rugby (along with the audience) know of the other "Simple" who is hiding in the closet. Added to the complications of rival lovers in this scene is a new subplot, in which an irate Frenchman vows to revenge himself on the cagey Welsh parson. The very thought of these two making "fritters of the English language" (as Falstaff will later say of Hugh) as they battle it out is sure to please an audience.

## ACT II – SCENE 1

**Summary**

Mrs. Page, then Mrs. Ford enters with the news that they have
received identical letters from Falstaff, pledging his love to each. Need-
less to say, they are both outraged. *Mrs. Page:* "One that is well-nigh
worn to pieces with age to show himself a young gallant"; *Mrs. Ford:* "I
shall think the worse of fat men as long as I have an eye to make
difference of men's liking" [tell the difference between men]. They
determine to "be revenged on him" and set off with Mistress Quickly
to lay the plot.

Their husbands arrive onstage, discussing what "a yoke of his
[Falstaff's] discarded men," Pistol and Nym, have told them concerning Falstaff's amorous plans for their "merry wives." Ford plans to pass
himself off as a man named "Brook" to Falstaff in order to get further
information.

As the scene ends, the subplot moves forward. Shallow reports
that "there is a fray to be fought between Sir Hugh the Welsh parson
and Caius the French doctor" and that they have been "appointed con-
trary [different] places" to meet for the duel. Page says that he would
"rather hear them scold [argue] than fight."

**Commentary**

Shakespeare differentiates between the two husbands – Page and
Ford – and, to a lesser extent, between the two wives in this scene.
Mrs. Page is openly contemptuous of Falstaff's scheme right from the
start, while Mrs. Ford worries about its consequences and seems fear-
ful at first even to tell her friend about Falstaff's letter. When Mrs.
Ford does speak, however, her scathing comments about Falstaff are
quite colorful:

> What tempest, I trow, threw this whale, with so
> many tuns of oil in his belly, ashore at Windsor? How
> shall I be revenged on him? I think the best way were
> to entertain him with hope, till the wicked fire of lust
> have melted him in his own grease.
>
> (64–68)

Perhaps Mrs. Ford's initial apprehension was justifiable, given the kind of person Ford turns out to be. His jealousy and his tendency to believe that his wife is a willing partner of Falstaff, contrasts sharply with Page's reaction to Falstaff:

> *Page:* If he should intend his voyage toward my wife,
> I would turn her loose to him; and what he gets
> more of her than sharp words, let it lie on my
> head.
> *Ford:* I do not misdoubt my wife, but I would be
> loath to turn them together. A man may be too
> confident.
>
> (188–92)

Ford's idea to disguise himself as another person – Brook – adds a final wrinkle to the plot's complications, whose working out will be the business of the rest of the play.

## ACT II – SCENE 2

### Summary

Pistol begs a loan from Falstaff; after all, it is *he* who usually takes the risks in their petty crimes. Falstaff reminds the lesser partner that it is only through his – Falstaff's – greater influence and connections that Pistol avoids failure. In typically pompous fashion, Falstaff asks, "Think'st thou I'll endanger my soul gratis?" His rationalization for his crooked ways echoes the Falstaff of *Henry IV, Part 1:* "Ay, I myself sometimes, leaving the fear of God on the left hand and hiding mine honor in necessity, am fain to shuffle, to hedge, and to lurch. . . ."

Mistress Quickly interrupts with the happy news that *both* Mrs. Page and Mrs. Ford are infatuated with the scholar knight, "The best courtier of them all, when the court lay at Windsor, could never have brought her [Mrs. Ford] to such a canary." Falstaff's ego swells at the idea of a successful conquest (or two!). As he addresses himself affectionately, now alone on stage, one imagines the comic effect that could be had if a large full-length mirror were present for him to peer into:

Will they yet look after thee?
Wilt thou, after the expense of so much money,
Be now a gainer? Good body, I thank thee.
Let them say 'tis grossly [a pun on "fat"] done;
So it be fairly done, no matter."

(145–49)

Disguised as "Mr. Brook," Ford solicits the aid of Falstaff in seducing Mrs. Ford (for the purpose of justifying his unfounded jealousy). The "bag of money" which he swings before Falstaff's nose is enough to convince this "gentleman of excellent breeding" to accept the project. "You shall, if you will, enjoy Ford's wife," Falstaff assures "Brook." Falstaff then hurls several gratuitous insults at Ford before the scene ends: "Hang him, mechanical salt-butter [vulgar, smelly] rogue!"

## Commentary

The multiple references to money give this scene its special edge. It opens with Falstaff haggling over money with someone he undoubtedly exploits with regularity. Virtually every character in the play has his part determined by his wealth (or lack of it). This is common enough in a farce of this kind, yet it reaches grotesque proportions in this scene. Ford (Brook) knows the great lure of hard cash to a nobleman fallen on hard times. Note the way he entices Falstaff:

There is money. Spend it, spend it;
Spend more; spend all I have.

(240–41)

Undoubtedly Ford waves real coins in front of Falstaff at this moment. One can imagine the impecunious knight's pleasure in fingering the silver. The final joke here, though, is on Ford himself, whose obsession with "property," one imagines, extends to his wife. His jealousy has actually distorted his vision of things to the point where he will risk actually having his wife dishonor herself in order to prove his (unfounded) jealousy. His language is almost that of a madman:

Page is an ass, a secure ass. He will trust his wife;

he will not be jealous. I will rather trust a Fleming with my butter, Parson Hugh the Welshman with my cheese, an Irishman with my aqua-vitae [whiskey] bottle, or a thief to walk my ambling gelding, than my wife with herself. Then she plots, then she ruminates, then she devises. And what they think in their hearts they may effect; they will break their hearts but they will effect. God be praised for my jealousy!"

(316–24)

His next action is to catch his wife "in the act" at "eleven o'clock the hour," as Falstaff has promised.

# ACT II – SCENE 3

## Summary

In a field near Windsor, Doctor Caius and his servant, John Rugby, have already waited beyond the appointed hour for Sir Hugh Evans. When Shallow arrives with several others, he muses that it is for the best that no duel has taken place, since it would "go against the hair of your profession"; that is, for a healer of bodies and a healer of souls to fight to the death would be wrong. Shallow, the Host of the Garter, Slender, Page, and Doctor Caius set off for the village of Frogmore, where Sir Hugh Evans is awaiting them.

## Commentary

Besides advancing the subplot, this scene offers the comic spectacle of John Rugby fending off his master Doctor Caius who, it seems, is a bit over-eager for a scrap:

> *Caius:* Take your rapier, Jack, I vill tell you how I
> vill kill him.
> *Rugby:* Alas, sir, I cannot fence.
> *Caius:* Villainy, take your rapier.

The Host of the Garter, who has arranged this absurd duel in the first place, seizes every opportunity to mock Doctor Caius' poor grasp of

the English language. He mischievously substitutes "adversary" for
"advocate."

> *Caius:* By gar, me dank you vor dat . . .
> *Host:* For the which I will be thy adversary toward
>        Anne Page. Said I well?
> *Caius:* By gar, 'tis good; vell said.

(94–97)

# ACT III – SCENES 1 & 2

### Summary

The scene shifts to Frogmore, where Hugh Evans vows to "knog
[Caius'] urinals about his knave's costard [head]." When he notices
Page, Slender, and Shallow on their way toward him, he quickly puts
on his gown and reads from his holy book. They notice the sword,
and Shallow asks, "What, the sword and the word [bible]! Do you study
them both, Master Parson?" Then Caius arrives, ripe for battle, and
Hugh Evans tries his best to pull him aside and postpone the duel:
"Pray you, let us not be laughingstocks to other men's humours." The
Host takes great pleasure in their embarrassment, commenting, "Peace,
I say, Gallia [Wales] and Gaul [France], French and Welsh, soul-curer
and body curer!" And then he admits that the whole ruse was his
private brainchild: "I have deceived you both: I have directed you to
wrong places." Left alone with his adversary, Hugh Evans proposes
to Caius a new revenge plot: ". . . let us knog or prains together to
be revenge on this same scall [scurvy fellow], scurvy, cogging [con-
niving] companion, the Host of the Garter."

In Scene 2, Ford comes across Mrs. Page in the company of
Falstaff's emissary, the young page Robin. This spurs his jealousy on,
and he tests her:

> *Ford:* I think if your husbands were dead, you two
>        [Robin and Mrs. Page] would marry.
> *Mrs. Page:* Be sure of that – two other husbands.

(14–15)

The company of duelists and witnesses arrives from Frogmore, and the debate continues as to which of Anne Page's various suitors is most fitting to have her hand. Page explains that he favors Master Slender, while his wife prefers Doctor Caius. When the Host of the Garter mentions the gentleman Master Fenton, Page adamantly refuses to hear of such a thing:

> The gentleman is of no having [has no property]. . . .
> The wealth I have waits on my consent, and my consent goes not that way.
>
> (72; 78–79)

## Commentary

The flow of these two scenes gives us an idea just how much this play belongs to the stage. In reading it, there is nothing remarkable or new, and the literary value of the writing is slim. On stage, however, the mounting confusion and visual high jinks would more than compensate. There is a virtual dance between Caius and Evans, the one eager to fight at all costs, and the other embarrassed by his predicament, first trying to hide behind his holy "cloth" and bible, then trying to explain to the French doctor (in a series of frantic asides) that it would be best to call the whole thing off. Then there is Slender. He has very little to say here, and he hardly needs to be present to advance the plot. His presence, however, as Shakespeare outlines it, is potentially highly comical. Apparently, his two encounters with Anne Page have utterly transformed him from a young (and slow-witted) sport, fit only to discuss such things as the finer qualities of local greyhounds, into a moonstruck lover. Earlier in the play, he was the picture of vagueness when he bowed to Shallow's proposal that he try to win Anne Page's hand; in the present scenes, Shakespeare has him totally enraptured by the very thought of the same woman. "Ah, sweet Anne Page!" is all he can say, which he does repeatedly, in perfect oblivion of the goings-on around him. The fact that Slender is an ass is indisputable; and that Mister Page is convinced that this is the man for his daughter is therefore all the more amazing.

Ford's peculiar madness is stressed in these scenes as well. He is positively gleeful at the thought of surprising his wife and Falstaff together:

Good plots! They are laid, and our revolted wives
share damnation together. Well, I will take him
[Falstaff], then torture my wife, pluck the borrowed
veil of modesty from the so-seeming Mistress Page,
divulge Page himself for a secure and willful Acteon
[cuckold]; and to these violent proceedings all my
neighbours shall cry aim [hurrah!]."

(39–45)

## ACT III – SCENE 3

### Summary

Falstaff steps into the trap set for him by Mrs. Page and Mrs. Ford.
"Have I caught thee, my heavenly jewel?" the fat knight croons to Mrs.
Ford upon arrival, only to find himself a few minutes later demean-
ingly transported out of her house in a "buck-basket" [a dirty linen
hamper] to avoid discovery by her husband. Ford is fooled as well,
since he fully expected to find the fat knight compromising his wife's
"honesty." For Mrs. Ford's part, the pleasure is a double one: "I know
not which pleases me better – that my husband is deceived, or Sir
John." The two women immediately plan a further adventure in order
to offer Falstaff "another hope, to betray him to another punishment."

Disappointed and embarrassed, Ford invites Page, Caius, and
Evans to a dinner which he has promised them. At the end of the
scene, Caius and Evans reaffirm their plan to be revenged on the Host.

### Commentary

Falstaff enters the scene; now he is "sweet Sir John," the over-
age, would-be courtly lover, spouting poetry and eager for a sexual
conquest. He exits this scene as a whale with so many "tuns of oil
in his belly," crammed into a basket which no doubt sags precariously
between its unfortunate bearers. Imagine the sight of Falstaff trying
to save his skin by squeezing into the basket:

> *Mrs. Ford:* He's too big to go in there. What shall I do?
> *Falstaff:* Let me see it, let me see it. O let me see it!
> I'll in, I'll in! Follow your friend's counsel. I'll in!

(142–44)

Shakespeare compounds the insult by strongly contrasting the language of Falstaff to the reality of his situation. References made to smelling "like Bucklersbury in simple-time" (the street in London where herbs were sold) are especially comical when one considers the stench of dirty linen under which Falstaff will soon find himself. Mrs. Ford extends the idea, no doubt hardly able to stifle her laughter, when she explains to Mrs. Page that Falstaff's extreme fear may cause him to loose his bowels, so that he'll be in a *real* need of ducking in ditch water, which they have instructed the servants to give him:

> *Mrs. Page:* What a taking [fright] was he in when
> your husband asked who was in the basket!
> *Mrs. Ford:* I am half afraid he will have need of wash-
> ing; so throwing him into the water will do him
> a benefit.
>
> (191–95)

Just as Falstaff is being lugged off-stage, Ford hesitates before the basket, but he does not inspect anything. The tension is exquisitely comic, and it intensifies when Ford hears the buzz-word "buck" [cuckold] uttered by his wife, albeit with a different meaning. One wonders if she puts stress on the word, however, in order to raise his hackles.

> *Mrs. Ford:* Why, what have you to do whither they
> bear it [the basket]? You were best meddle with
> buck-washing!
> *Ford:* Buck? I would I could wash myself of the buck
> [horned animal – *i.e.,* cuckold]! Buck, buck buck!
> Ay, buck; I warrant you, buck – and of the season
> too, it shall appear.
>
> (163–69)

Ford's extreme reaction and Falstaff's extreme debasement highlight the scene.

# ACT III – SCENES 4 & 5

**Summary**

Fenton assures Anne Page that he truly loves her, although he admits her "father's wealth/ Was the first motive that I wooed thee." Their conversation ends abruptly when Slender arrives. Anne despairingly speaks her thoughts on the matter in an aside:

> This is my father's choice. O what a world of vile,
> ill-favoured faults looks handsome in three hundred
> pounds a year.
>
> (31–33)

Slender attempts to engage Anne in small talk for a few moments, but Mrs. Page and Mistress Quickly suddenly join them. Anne's mother's choice of a suitor is equally distasteful, and when Quickly refers to her "Master Doctor" as a possible husband, Anne unequivocally refuses:

> Alas, I had rather be set quick i' th' earth
> And bowled to death with turnips.
>
> (90–91)

Scene 4 ends with Mistress Quickly on stage, determined to "do what I can for them all three"–that is, whatever she can do for the potential husbands, for a *price!* (She has just taken a ring and a bribe to deliver the ring to Anne from Fenton.)

In Scene 5, Falstaff guzzles wine to counter the effect of his dousing in the river, both the wet of it and the horror of it. As he explains,

> And you may know by my size that I have a kind
> of alacrity in sinking. If the bottom were as deep as
> hell, I should down. . . . I should have been a moun-
> tain of mummy [dead flesh].
>
> (11–13; 18)

The sight of Master Brook (Ford in disguise) cheers Falstaff into considering another try with Mrs. Ford: "I like his money well." The scene ends as Ford, fuming with anger at having been tricked with the buck-basket (as Falstaff just explained), determines to catch the "lecher" the next time.

## Commentary

Fenton and Anne Page are the normative characters in the comedy. Although ruled at first by the same motivations as the rest of the world, Fenton honestly explains that he would now love Anne — even if he didn't need her money. The audience, conventionally, accepts this as a fact and therefore turns its keener attention to the idiocies of the alternate lovers. The scene between Anne Page and Slender is a classic piece of comedy. From previous scenes, we know that Slender is taken with the idea of marrying Anne Page, yet once he is with her, he freezes and becomes a tongue-tied adolescent. Shallow encourages the small talk between them, but Slender can barely function:

> *Shallow:* She's coming; to her, coz. O boy, thou hadst
> a father!
> *Slender:* I had a father, Mistress Anne [here, one
> imagines a pause, then an exasperated pitch for
> help]; my uncle can tell you good jests of him.
> Pray you, uncle, tell Mistress Anne the jest how
> my father stole two geese out of a pen, good
> uncle.
> *Shallow:* Mistress Anne, my cousin loves you.
> *Slender:* Ay, that I do. . . .
> *Anne:* Good Master Shallow, let him woo for himself.
>
> (36–43; 51)

To top this comic turn, Slender reverts to his old self (or at least his old words) when he tells Anne that the whole idea was hatched by his uncle and her father in the first place. Anything, it seems, is preferable to poor Slender than having to come face-to-face with such a young, energetic woman!

Falstaff's description of his misadventure ranks among the richest displays of language in the play. He has just consumed immense quantities of wine in a short period, and he now unloads his woeful tale on

Master Brook/Ford. Of course, Ford has very mixed emotions here. Undoubtedly he loves the idea of Falstaff's smelly demise; on the other hand, he is furious at having been duped himself. He is also worried that Falstaff won't be willing to give it another try. One must read the following speech in the spirit of pompous (and theatrical) injured dignity which only a Falstaff can muster:

> I suffered the pangs of three several deaths: first, an intolerable fright to be detected with [by] a jealous rotten bell-wether [cuckold]; next, to be compassed like a good bilbo [flexed sword] in the circumference of a peck, hilt to point, heel to head; and then, to be stopp'd in, like a strong distillation, with stinking clothes that fretted in their own grease. Think of that, a man of my kidney [temperament] – think of that – that am as subject to heat as butter; a man of continued dissolution and thaw. It was a miracle to 'scape suffocation. And in the height of this bath, when I was more than half stewed in grease, like a Dutch dish, to be thrown into the Thames, and cooled, glowing hot, in that surge, like a horseshoe. Think of that – hissing hot – think of that, Master Brook!

(109–23)

Remember that Falstaff is also putting on a performance here for a fee. He wants Brook to know the full extent of the suffering he has endured "to bring this woman to evil for your good." Each of them is eager beyond all previous measure to see the plot succeed next time – one out of greed, the other because of jealousy.

## ACT IV – SCENE 1

### Summary

Mrs. Page asks Sir Hugh Evans to test her son William in his Latin grammatical inflections. While Sir Hugh does so, Mistress Quickly repeatedly interrupts with absurd comments and off-color remarks, deriving from unintentional puns on the Latin words which William recites.

64

## Commentary

This scene has absolutely nothing to do with the plot of the play, and various commentators have suggested that Shakespeare added it as an amusement for an educated audience at a special performance, since only they would understand the Latin puns. That is debatable, however, since even the middle class would have had enough schooling (as had William in the play) to catch most of the references. The scene serves at least the technical function of allowing bridging action between Falstaff's resolve to try his luck again with Mrs. Ford, and his arrival at her house. Furthermore, what transpires is amusing in itself (or was, for an audience that understood Latin), as we witness a poor schoolboy caught between a pedant and a daffy woman while he tries to do his lessons. When William hears "focative case" [vocative, in Welsh dialect], he answers "O – 'vocatino, O'" – in all innocence! But Quickly and a sophisticated audience know that "case" also means "pudenda," making the "O" an unintentional, obscene pun.

# ACT IV – SCENES 2–4

## Summary

The wives engineer a second narrow escape for Falstaff from the furious Ford, this time as "the witch of Brainford," Mrs. Ford's maid's fat aunt, the mere sight of whom sends Ford into a rage. Falstaff submits to disguising himself as a woman so that he can evade Ford and the crowd which accompanies him. To escape, however, he must first endure a cudgeling:

> *Ford:* I'll 'prat' [best] her. Out of my door, you witch,
> you hag, you baggage, you polecat, you ronyon!
> Out, out!
>
> (194–95)

Still asserting that his "jealousy is reasonable," Ford searches for evidence of his wife's unfaithfulness – again in vain.

The "merry wives" determine to carry on their harrassment of John Falstaff, if their husbands so wish. In Scene 4, Ford begs pardon of his wife for his being such a fool – "I rather will suspect the sun with cold/ Than thee with wantonness" – and the group decides to have one last sport at Falstaff's expense. A local folk tale has it that "Herne the Hunter," many years ago a gamekeeper in Windsor Forest, haunts the area in wintertime, blighting the trees and bewitching the cattle. He walks around an old oak tree, wearing "great ragg'd horns," and shaking a chain "in a most hideous and dreadful manner." The plan is to induce Falstaff to meet both women at Herne's oak, wearing horns on his head and disguised as the ancient gamekeeper. The rest of the company will surprise him and "mock him home to Windsor." Before the scene ends, both Page and Mrs. Page separately reveal (in asides) that they will help their daughter sneak off to marry each one's favorite suitor, respectively Slender and Doctor Caius.

Scene 3 is an interlude in which Bardolph tells the Host of the Garter Inn about the arrival of a German duke. Three of his compatriots need to hire horses to go meet him. The Host emphasizes that he will "make them pay; I'll sauce them."

## Commentary

The merry pace of the farce continues here, showing an absurd disguising of Falstaff as a fat witch and promising yet another, Falstaff horned like a beast, as "Herne the Hunter." There is a gleeful sense of mischief in Mrs. Page and Mrs. Ford's actions, which dictates the tone of the scenes. As Mrs. Page puts it, "We'll leave a proof by that which we will do/ Wives may be merry, and yet honest too." In order to keep the wives' high spirits on this side of sadism and to break the monotony, Shakespeare draws the husbands into the final plot to unmask Falstaff. Indeed, there is something almost festive about the two families' plans for the midnight plot.

> *Mrs. Page:* Nan Page, my daughter, and my little son,
> and three or four more of their growth, we'll
> dress like urchins, ouphes [elves], and fairies,
> green and white, with rounds of waxen tapers
> on their heads, and rattles in their hands. Upon
> a sudden, as Falstaff, she and I are newly met.
> . . . Let them all encircle him about. And, fairy-
> like, to pinch the unclean knight.
> (47–52; 56–57)

Even Mrs. Page and her benevolent husband have blind spots when it comes to the marriage of their daughter Anne. The mother's desire for social connections ("friends potent at court") spurs her on to propose a secret wedding with Doctor Caius; and, as before, Mr. Page is intent on having the financially sound "Master Slender steal my Nan away." Folly is not the sole property of Falstaff in this play.

## ACT IV – SCENES 5 & 6

### Summary

Slender has sent his man Simple to seek the advice of the "Witch of Brainford" on two matters: (1) a chain which he suspects Nym to have stolen and (2) the prospects of his marrying Anne Page. Falstaff explains that the fat woman has just left, but not before they discussed these very things. Stupidly satisfied that his master will be pleased to hear that Anne Page "might or might not" accept Slender, Simple leaves. Next, we learn of the Host's ill-fortune. His horses have been stolen by "three cozen-Germans." Falstaff, in a depressed state himself, welcomes the news of anyone else's misery: "I would all the world might be cozened, for I have been cozened [cheated] and beaten too." Quickly lures Falstaff to his chamber with a letter which promises a means of bringing him together with "two parties." He follows her.

Fenton solicits the aid of the Host in procuring Anne Page as his wife. He explains her mother's and father's separate plans to marry her to men of *their* choice.

> *Host:* Which means she to deceive, father or mother?
> *Fenton:* Both, my good Host, to go along with me.
>
> (46–47)

The Host agrees to help by hiring a priest and waiting in an appointed spot.

### Commentary

Falstaff is the largest figure in *The Merry Wives of Windsor* in every imaginable way. What a colossal ego it must take to find oneself thwarted twice in secret assignations with a woman – only to be seduced by the idea of having one's way with two women at a time! The fun is amplified by the hypocrisy of the perpetrator. Falstaff is loved because he is incorrigible: "Well, if my wind were but long enough to say my prayers, I would repent." References to the petty idiocies of characters such as Slender and to the more ordinary machinations of Evans (who, with Caius, probably stole the Host's horses) make Falstaff seem even a greater (while lesser) character.

The Fenton episode is purely traditional in inspiration: in romantic comedy, true love must find its way to fruition.

## ACT V – SCENES 1–5

### Summary

Falstaff promises Master Brook some "wonders" at midnight by Herne's oak; Page reminds Slender that his daughter will be waiting; and Mrs. Page reassures Caius that Anne Page is ready to be swept away "to the deanery" (to be married); Hugh Evans, disguised as a satyr, calls "Trib, trib [trip], fairies" and leads a troop of revelers to their rendezvous in Windsor Park. So much for the first four scenes of the final act of *The Merry Wives of Windsor*.

Scene 5 is the climax of the play. Horns on his head, Falstaff calls on "the hot-blooded gods" to assist him. He is virtually licking his lips in anticipation when the two women appear. He "magnanimously" proposes to both of them: "Divide me like a bribed [filched] buck, each a haunch." Immediately the general hubub of the assembled "fairies" is heard, and the two women run off, leaving Falstaff believing that hell itself has had a hand in preventing his sexual mischief these three times: "I think the devil will not have me damned, lest the oil that's in me should set hell on fire. He would never else cross me thus."

Falstaff throws himself down but is discovered (hardly surprising!) by the satyr (Evans) and the Fairy Queen (Quickly). They put him to the test of chastity: touching his "finger end" with fire. When he cries out in pain, the lecher is denounced:

> Corrupt, corrupt, and tainted in desire!
> About him, fairies, sing a scornful rhyme;
> And, as you trip, still pinch him to your time.

(94–96)

When all decide to end the jest, Falstaff is nonplussed: "I do begin to perceive that I am made an ass." Both Slender and Doctor Caius arrive before long and announce that they have been tricked into running off with *boys,* whom they mistook for Anne Page. To end the play, the newly married couple, Master Fenton and Anne Page, explain themselves:

> The truth is, she and I, long since contracted, are now
> so
> Sure [wedded] that nothing can dissolve us.
>
> (234–35)

All present cheer the outcome and follow Mrs. Page:

> Heaven give you [Anne and Fenton] many, many
> merry days!
> Good husband, let us every one go home,
> And laugh this sport o'er by a country fire;
> Sir John and all.
>
> (254–57)

## Commentary

A change in style marks the very last scene of the play. The verse, the elaborate costumes, and the ceremonial nature of the events involving the "fairy kingdom" in the harrassment and final exposure of Falstaff resemble a courtly masque in form. The masque was a courtly entertainment that stressed allegorical figures, splendid costuming, and dancing, in which audience members were encouraged to participate. It highlighted special occasions at court. Many scholars associate *The Merry Wives of Windsor* (certainly this part of it) with the installation of new members into the honored Order of the Garter by Queen Elizabeth in May, 1597. (Indeed, George Carey, the second Lord Hunsdon and a favorite of the Queen, was installed on that occasion.) He was also the patron of Shakespeare's company of actors at the time. When Mistress Quickly, incongruously decked out as the Fairy Queen, instructs the fairy troupe to search the area for any creatures unfit to· be present, she makes direct references to Windsor and to the chapel of St. George, where the Knights of the Garter had their stalls.

*Quickly:* About, about.
      Search Windsor Castle, elves, within and out.
      Strew good luck, ouphes, on every sacred room,
      That it may stand till the perpetual doom,
      In state as wholesome as in state 'tis fit,
      Worthy the owner, and the owner it.
      The several chairs of order [of the Garter] look
          you scour
      With juice of balm and every precious flower.

                        (59–66)

Regardless of these historical details, the final scene offers a splendid and fantastical ending to the comedy. Major characters are transformed and amazed, one after the other. Falstaff has become a horned beast, then an "ass," by his own admittance. His physical torment is real when they "put tapers to his fingers," but one imagines the humiliation which he endures goes beyond that pain: "Have I lived to stand at the taunt of one that makes fritters of English [that is, of Hugh Evans, the Welshman]?"

In the spirit of this good-natured farce, no resistance is offered to the final piece of trickery which results in a perfect matrimonial match between Fenton and Anne Page. General applause and a "country fire" round out the play, which includes *all* of the characters in its final celebration.

## QUESTIONS FOR REVIEW

1. This play is the only one in the Shakespearean canon which deals with contemporary England as such. Identify aspects of the language which would lead you to call it a "realistic" play.

2. What significance do the various disguises and exotic costumings have in the play?

3. What is a courtly masque and how does the tradition of the masque function in the play?

4. Would it be fair to say that everyone in the play is a fool, or a potential fool?

5. What is a farce? To what extent is *The Merry Wives of Windsor* a farce?

6. Describe the main features of Falstaff's language.

7. Some scholars have felt that the Falstaff of *The Merry Wives of Windsor* is infinitely inferior to the character we know from the *Henry IV* plays. Do you agree?

8. Does this play show signs of hasty composition? Where?

9. Look carefully at Act III, Scene 3, and describe a possible staging of the "buck-basket" incident. What happens between the lines uttered during the concealment and those delivered during the transport of Falstaff off-stage?

10. Hardly a character in the play is unaffected by wealth, or the lack of it. How does each one's financial status influence his/her behavior?

## SELECTED BIBLIOGRAPHY

ADAMS, JOSEPH QUINCY. *A Life of William Shakespeare.* New York: Houghton-Mifflin Co., 1923.

ALEXANDER, PETER. *Shakespeare.* London: Oxford University Press, 1964.

BARBER, C. L. *Shakespeare's Festive Comedy.* Princeton: Princeton University Press, 1959.

BENTLEY, GERALD EADES. *Shakespeare, a Biographical Handbook.* Theobold Lewis, ed. New Haven: Yale University Press, 1961.

BETHELL, S. L. *Shakespeare and the Popular Tradition.* London: King and Staples, 1944.

BROWN, JOHN RUSSELL. *Shakespeare and His Comedies.* London: Methuen and Co., 1957.

CLEMEN, WOLFGANG. *The Development of Shakespeare's Imagery.* London: Methuen and Co., 1951.

CRAIG, HARDIN. *An Interpretation of Shakespeare.* New York: Dryden Press, 1948.

ELLIS-FERMOR, UNA M. *Shakespeare the Dramatist.* London: Geoffrey Cumberlege, 1948.

PALMER, JOHN. *Comic Characters of Shakespeare.* London: The Macmillan Company, 1946.

PARROTT, THOMAS MARC. *Shakespearean Comedy.* New York: Oxford University Press, 1949.

PRIESTLEY, J. B. *The English Comic Characters.* London: The Bodley Head, 1925; reprinted 1963.

PURDOM, C. B. *What Happens in Shakespeare.* London: John Baker, 1963.

SITWELL, EDITH. *A Notebook on William Shakespeare.* London: Oxford University Press, 1928.

WATKINS, RONALD. *Moonlight at the Globe.* London: Michael Joseph, 1946.

WELSFORD, ENID. *The Court Masque.* Cambridge: University Press, 1927.

WILSON, J. DOVER. *The Essential Shakespeare.* New York: Cambridge University Press, 1932.

# NOTES